ST. VINCENT HEALTHCARE

A part of Billings since 1898 when the first Sisters of Charity of Leavenworth responded to a call to build a hospital, St. Vincent Healthcare has been a part of the fabric of the community, growing, changing, and adapting to the needs of the people who call Billings and the region home.

Today, St. Vincent Healthcare has a medical staff of over 420 physicians, serving a four-state area with a population of over 1 million. Services include comprehensive cancer care, orthopedics including the Montana Joint Center, an award-winning cardiovascular program, neurosciences, women's and children's services including a pediatric ICU with intensivists on call 24 hours a day 7 days a week, and surgical services including bariatric surgery.

A part of the community since the beginning, St. Vincent Healthcare has 2,200 employees, including over 700 nurses. The commitment runs deep, in the care the employees provide to patients and in the contributions St. Vincent Healthcare makes to the greater community. Each year, millions of dollars in charity care are provided to those in need of financial assistance, and local organizations serving the needs of the community receive support from St. Vincent Healthcare in the form of donations and sponsorships.

In the spirit of the early Sisters who heeded the call and built Billings first hospital, St. Vincent Healthcare continues provide excellent, quality healthcare.

Learn more about St. Vincent Healthcare and the commitment to Quality, visit www.svh-mt.org.

Billings

MONTANA'S TRAILHEAD

 BY SUE HART

DEDICATION

With love and respect to all those who have contributed to the building of community in Billings over the last 127 years—and a challenge to those who will follow to keep our city true to the values and dreams of those who first settled here and all those since who have called Billings home.

TITLE PAGE PHOTO: The statue of Frederick Billings, for whom the town is named, stands on the grounds of the Western Heritage Center, originally the Parmly Billings Memorial Library. Mike Capser created the sculpture.
ROB MASSEE

Copyright © 2009 by Sue Hart

All rights reserved, including the right to reproduce this work in any form whatsoever without permission in writing from the publisher, except for brief passages in connection with a review. For information, please write:

The Donning Company Publishers
184 Business Park Drive, Suite 206
Virginia Beach, VA 23462

Steve Mull, General Manager
Barbara Buchanan, Office Manager
Pamela Koch, Senior Editor
Jennifer Penaflor, Graphic Designer
Derek Eley, Imaging Artist
Debby Dowell, Project Research Coordinator
Tonya Hannink, Marketing Specialist
Pamela Engelhard, Marketing Advisor

Ed Williams, Project Director

Library of Congress Cataloging-in-Publication Data

Hart, Sue (Suzanne)
  Billings : Montana's trailhead / by Sue Hart.
    p. cm.
  Includes bibliographical references and index.
  ISBN 978-1-57864-514-5 (hard cover : alk. paper)
  1. Billings (Mont.)—History. 2. Billings (Mont.)—History—Pictorial works. 3. Billings (Mont.)—Economic conditions. I. Title.
  F739.B5H37 2008
  978.6'39--dc22
                            2008023945

Printed in the United States of America at Walsworth Publishing Company

TABLE OF contents

FOREWORD 6

PREFACE 7

ACKNOWLEDGMENTS 8

CHAPTER ONE 8
Billings in the Nineteenth Century, 1882–1899

CHAPTER TWO 26
Billings in the Early Twentieth Century, 1900–1920

CHAPTER THREE 46
Billings in the 1920s and '30s

CHAPTER FOUR 68
Billings in the 1940s and '50s

CHAPTER FIVE 84
Billings in the 1960s and '70s

CHAPTER SIX 98
Billings in the 1980s and '90s

CHAPTER SEVEN 116
Billings in the Twenty-first Century

NOTES 140

BIBLIOGRAPHY 142

INDEX 143

ABOUT THE AUTHOR 144

Welcome to Montana's Trailhead. Billings is a place of forever views, a place rich in history, a place of vibrant growth, and a place with the adventure of the untamed wilderness next door.

Nowhere is the great outdoors quite as great as it is here. The north and east sides of the city are framed by gorgeous 400-foot sandstone Rimrocks while the south meets the legendary, free-flowing Yellowstone River. Here, the plains meet the mountains, and the view of seven mountain ranges from atop the Rimrocks will take your breath away. Take in the Pryors, Big Horns, Bull, Snowy, Crazy, Absaroka, and Beartooth mountains from one serene spot. Beyond our local limits, both Yellowstone National Park and Glacier National Park are just a scenic drive away. With all of these mysteries of nature right in our backyard, it goes without saying that Billings is full of people who love to experience the outdoors. Hunting, fishing, rafting, biking, camping, horseback riding, snowmobiling, geocaching, skiing, and snowboarding are all a way of life. Billings is the perfect place to breathe deep and spend some time outside.

Billings is brimming with Western heritage. Mountain men, gunslingers, cattle barons, railroad tycoons, and famous (or infamous) outlaws were all a part of writing Billings' early history. Just a short drive away is the place where General Custer fought the Sioux and Cheyenne and where Sitting Bull and Crazy Horse led their people to victories and through struggles. That same adventurous spirit was present when William Clark left his signature nearby, Calamity Jane raised a ruckus, and Charles Lindbergh performed as a barnstorming aviator. In and near Billings, you will walk in the footsteps of the legends of the West.

Beyond the Western charm and outdoor leisure opportunities, Billings is a great place to live, learn, work, and play because of its resilient economy, medical and educational opportunities, and cultural attractions. As the largest city in a 500-mile radius, Billings is the center of progressive regional commerce. Billings' medical corridor provides the best healthcare services available in a four-state region. Home to Montana State University Billings, the MSUB College of Technology, and Rocky Mountain College, Billings offers a full-spectrum of educational options on every learning level. With great restaurants, museums, theatres, festivals, and local artists, Billings is the cultural hub of the region. Billings connects you to warm, genuine, hardworking people who possess a perspective on life that embraces our Western heritage. Inherently individual, we take the time to look you in the eye and make you feel at home.

Billings is Montana's Trailhead. From here, your trail can take you back in time or to the top of the world, anywhere or nowhere at all. So, weigh the possibilities, get ready for the trek of a lifetime, and then decide…where ya headin'.

John Brewer CAE, President & CEO
Billings Chamber of Commerce/Convention & Visitors Bureau

preface

At a little over 125 years old, Billings, Montana, has seen its share of up and downs, of success and failure, of good fortune and bad. Nicknamed "The Magic City" from its inception because of its rapid growth, it suffered setbacks in the form of fire, floods, and farm failures, yet it continued to build on its strengths and rise above its misfortunes, as befits the city that is Montana's Trailhead. The magic has never left this "Star of the Big Sky Country," and we hope it never will.

ACKNOWLEDGMENTS

Western Heritage Center

The Montana Room, Parmly Billings Library

Montana State University Billings Library

Department of English & Philosophy, Montana State University Billings

SPECIAL THANKS TO

My Family

Rob Massee

Dennis Schuld

Darrel Williams

Kevin Kooistra-Manning

Julie Dial

LaVonne Madden

Noel Hawke

Mary Kay Latta

Bonnie Herminghaus

Mary Hawkins

Zoe Kilbourne

Pamela Koch, Excellent & Patient Editor

Jennifer Penaflor, Wonderful Graphic Designer

Chapter ONE
BILLINGS IN THE NINETEENTH CENTURY, 1882–1899

DESTINATION: BILLINGS, MONTANA

Billings MONTANA'S TRAILHEAD

Chances are that the first white settlers in the Billings area were unaware of the area's ancient past that accounts for many of its most prominent features, including the sandstone cliffs known as the Rimrocks, which rise most dramatically on the northern edge of the city, or of its earliest human inhabitants, some of whom foresaw the settlement of this area and the establishment of this community.

The earliest "residents" where Billings is located were not humans, but aquatic creatures living in a Mesozoic Period sea bounded by the Rimrocks, the top of which served as a beach. (Today, young people, especially students at Rocky Mountain College and Montana State University Billings, both located at the base of the Rims, often refer to "Rimrock Beach," the ideal place to get an early suntan every summer.)

Throughout the early periods of glacial and aquatic activity, this area was home to sea creatures, such as snails and mollusks, and, in warmer periods, dinosaurs and other large mammals. And then, according to anthropologist Adrian Heidenreich, came the earliest humans on this part of the continent: "Indians first entered Montana some 12,000 years ago, during the Paleo-Indian or Early Prehistoric period when they hunted mammoths and giant bison."[1]

The first confirmed interaction between whites and Indians in the Billings area in May of 1823 did not end well for a party of white trappers led by Michael Immel and Robert Jones of the Missouri Fur Company. The trappers were ambushed by a large number of Blackfeet when traveling through a narrow gap in the Rimrocks, and Immel, Jones, and five others were killed. It is believed that theirs were the seven skulls uncovered when a large boulder was blasted as part of a road-building project shortly

When Billings members of the American Railway Union went on strike in 1894, soldiers stationed at Fort Custer were brought in to protect the community's infrastructure such as bridges and tunnels that management feared might be destroyed by the strikers. Apparently, Calamity Jane couldn't resist a man (or men) in uniform and dressed up in ladylike attire to visit with the troopers. WESTERN HERITAGE CENTER

after the turn of the twentieth century. Billings historian Joyce Jensen notes in her *Pieces & Places of Billings History*, "No accounts mention a burial; but the next year some of the survivors were in the same area and could have buried the remains."[2]

Crow historian Lawrence Flat Lip cites three incidents of Indian visions foretelling the settlement that was to become Billings: Crow Chief Long Hair, who lived in the 1700s, told his followers about the coming of a new civilization, and urged them to accept the "great changes" that would come about as a result; Bell Rock and Little Head, while fasting on the Rimrocks, saw bright lights shining into the night sky from the current site of Billings; and the great Chief Plenty Coups saw the buffalo swallowed up by the earth and replaced by cattle.[3]

BILLINGS BEGINS

Despite its frontier nature—Billings was, at first, just a collection of tents and ramshackle wooden structures that were hardly more than lean-tos—it did not take long for the new community to establish itself as an up-and-coming modern city. Billings had electricity by 1887 and telephones by 1895. It also had a number of business and professional men, drawn west, no doubt, by the same sense of adventure and promise of success that lured early mountain men, traders, pioneers, and homesteaders to abandon their settled home communities and venture west.

It had not taken long for Coulson, its nearby predecessor, to establish a Boot Hill cemetery at the foot of the Rims, and in its early years, several Billings residents or passersby were also buried there. Both Coulson and early Billings were rather rough and raw frontier communities, and that meant they drew adventure seekers, outlaws, the fiddle-footed, and those who catered to such a clientele. It took Billings a few years to outgrow its rather boisterous—and at times bawdy—beginnings. In fact, when the community's first hospital opened in 1899, seventeen years after the city's founding, the leading cause for admittance of patients was "gunshot wounds," followed by such ailments as frozen hands and feet, alcoholism or

Coulson was built along the Yellowstone River in 1877. Alkali Creek, in the foreground, used to run along the base of the Rims by the Fairgrounds before it was diverted north of the MetraPark parking lot in the 1970s. WESTERN HERITAGE CENTER

other medical problems brought on by excessive drinking, railroad accidents, and snakebites. Typhoid was a constant threat, and outbreaks reached epidemic status at times. Records also show cases of people being "kicked by a horse," "run over by wagon," or admitted as "morphine fiend."[4]

Even so, by the time proprietors of businesses and dwellers in Coulson had packed up their tents or moved their wooden structures to the new city of Billings, residents of the area were already predicting a great future for the new community. Issues of the *Billings Herald* in 1882 reflect the

The *Billings Herald* office, operated by publisher Edward Bromley and Alexander Devine, had plenty of room for expansion in 1882. WESTERN HERITAGE CENTER

Yellowstone Kelly, military scout in the 1870s, chose Montana as his final resting place. Billings civic leaders jumped at the chance to have the famous frontiersman's body brought here for burial atop the Rimrocks—even though it meant keeping the body on ice for six months before he could be interred. WESTERN HERITAGE CENTER

optimism of residents and the promise seen by all who visited the Magic City, so named for its rapid growth.

The *Herald*'s front pages usually carried more advertising than news, but the ads that ran speak eloquently of the promise of the new community. Many touted real estate opportunities: "Van Cleve & Worley, Real Estate Surveying and Insurance"; "Van Cleve and Wadsworth, Business & Residential Lots in Billings and in McAdow Addition"; "Benton, Wells, & Co., 100 of the choicest business and residence lots for sale."[5]

There were also a number of purveyors of needed items for those setting up a household. CW Thompson & Bro offered general merchandise, including groceries, clothing, glassware, crockery, boots, shoes, and notions. Johnson & Stoneman were dealers in staples or fancy groceries and provisions, and promised choice lines of the finest goods in the territory; their specialties included canned fruits, canned meats, canned fish, and canned vegetables. For those special events, Asa Fisher, wholesale dealer in wines, liquors, and cigars, offered Val Blatz's Export Lager Beer. Not to be outdone, Jas. Muldowney & John W. Smith, proprietors of The Florence on Montana Avenue, touted their imported wines, liquors, and cigars—a specialty. They also stocked the most popular brands of domestic goods, which, they promised, were "always in stock."[6]

Some diehards remained in Coulson—which could be reached by streetcars of the horse-drawn variety—and they, too, advertised in the *Herald*, including P. W. McAdow, founder of that small community, who offered flour and nails and bottled wines, liquors, and cordials.

Local hotels also advertised their presence in town. Visitors who arrived to look over the new community could check in at the National Hotel or enjoy the amenities of the Best Hotel, among others.

CHAPTER ONE BILLINGS IN THE NINETEENTH CENTURY, 1882–1899

Luther "Yellowstone" Kelly's grave today. ROB MASSEE

"Liver Eating" Johnson, famous for an event that may or may not have taken place (the eating of a liver taken from an Indian killed in a clash with soldiers and scouts) served as a police officer in early Billings. WESTERN HERITAGE CENTER

Residents and visitors did not lack for entertainment in early Billings. In July of 1882, a scant four months after the city was founded, "a full opera company carrying their own scenery" was coming to town to perform *The Magic Doll*, a presentation that offered "Mirth! Music! Fun!" and "Comical Situations"—all for a general admission price of $1.00, or, for the more prosperous, a reserved seat at $1.25.[7]

By fall, "one of the most pleasant and enjoyable social entertainments . . . since the inception of the town," according to the *Billings Herald* of October 8, was held at the Windsor Hotel. This first in a series of "social dances given by the Billings Social Club came off with the greatest éclat," according to the *Herald* account. "Over 20 couples were present and the general tone of the assembly was such as would do credit to a gathering of the elite in an old and prosperous town. Ladies and gentlemen appeared in the evening dress of society, where five months since there was scarcely a trace of the civilization which now manifests itself."[8]

That "civilization" was praised just a few days later when Colonel Lounsbury, the editor of the Bismarck, North Dakota, *Tribune*, offered his view on "Billings, the magic city," in the *Herald* of October 12:

It has indeed sprung up as if by magic, and is today the best abused and least appreciated point on the line of the Northern Pacific . . .

13

> In March last Billings was born and named in honor of Frederick Billings, one of the leading spirits of the Northern Pacific . . . He takes a deep personal interest in this city, named for him, and will not suffer its interests to languish, if capital in improvements will be of service.
>
> By actual count Billings now has 217 buildings where only a little over six months ago there were none. The railroad company is erecting an extensive roundhouse; at present eleven stalls, covering, however, only one-fourth of the plan. Shops to match will immediately be built. [Six hundred and fifty thousand bricks were contracted for] . . . the bricks are of dark red and good quality. They are using a hard blue sandstone from Lake Superior for trimming. Several brick buildings have already been built. Herman Clark, who owns a brickyard, is encouraging use in every way possible.
>
> Clark believes that at Billings can be built up one of the best wholesale points in the West.
>
> Every promise made to investors by the townsite company is being fulfilled.[9]

Obviously, for the most part settlers in Billings were business-minded, family- and community-oriented men who arrived with their wives and children and were determined to see their chosen hometown grow and prosper. These men—and often their wives, as well—had much to do with the fulfillment of the promise that they saw in this new and, in many ways, still raw frontier town. It is to that group of early residents the people of Billings today owe thanks, not only for the development of their community, but also for the foresight and generosity of many of those early settlers who provided not only employment possibilities, but also cultural, educational, and recreational opportunities that continue to enrich this area today.

While a good many solid citizens contributed to this community in large and small ways, some early residents are revered for their foresight and contributions to the building and betterment of Billings. And there are others who, during this same period, provided amusement—and sometimes amazement—over their misbehavior.

The wife of one of the early mayors of Billings, Mrs. Edgar B. Camp, whose husband was in office in 1888 and '89, recognized the potential of the bustling community Billings had become in just a few years and urged her husband to rename North Twenty-eighth Street "Broadway" because she thought such an up-and-coming community should have a street name that reflected its importance. Today, both the North Twenty-eighth Street and the North Broadway designations are used.

Among the prominent men in early Billings were P. B. Moss, Henry Rowley, I. D. O'Donnell, Charlie Bair, A. L. Babcock, and the Yegen brothers, Christian and Peter. Moss moved to Billings from Missouri in 1892, became president of the First National Bank, invested in agricultural and livestock ventures (he once ran some 80,000 head of sheep in partnership with T. A. Snidow) and in the sugar beet factory, founded the *Billings Evening Journal*, purchased *The Scientific Farmer* publication and moved its headquarters to Billings, and invested in a heating business, which kept a major portion of downtown comfortable in cold weather by sending hot water through a series of tunnels, and in an early telephone exchange. He built the Northern Hotel in partnership with Rowley and built a $105,000 twenty-eight-room family home on land that was then in the country west of town. That home, now known as the Moss Mansion House Museum, has been preserved almost exactly as it was when the family lived there.

H. L. Rowley came to Billings as a civil engineer for the Northern Pacific in 1880 and stayed on to become a prominent business leader in the community. He invested in both agricultural and construction projects, such as the original Northern Hotel.

I. D. O'Donnell came to Montana as a young man, and after some time spent on a ranch near Lewistown where he met Parmly Billings and Edward Bailey, he moved to Billings. Although many historical accounts credit O'Donnell with the construction of the Big Ditch that flows through Billings and provides irrigation water for several agricultural areas, he was not involved with the ditch company until well after its initial construction, serving as superintendent of the Big Ditch Company beginning in 1900. (H. W. Rowley was actually the engineer in charge of construction of the canal.) O'Donnell also operated Hesper Farm, which he purchased from E. G. Bailey. On his farm he experimented with various crops, including alfalfa, which had been raised on the property by the first owner, Benjamin Shuart, and sugar beets, which flourished. He was sometimes called the Alfalfa King, but it was his sugar beet venture that interested other area farmers in that crop. O'Donnell became a strong advocate for and investor in the building of the sugar beet processing plant in Billings, a business that is still an important factor in the Billings economy. (In 2007, it celebrated its one-hundredth anniversary.) His interest in water use continued, and his reputation and expertise in that field led to his being named supervisor of all United States Reclamation projects in the seventeen western states by the Secretary of the Interior in 1914. In 1919, *The Country Gentleman* named him Montana's No. 1 Farmer.

O'Donnell was also instrumental in starting the Yellowstone Fair Association, a venture that provided stock and crop growers an opportunity to show off their products to city dwellers, and gave everyone a chance to enjoy a relaxed social gathering with events for every age group. At the first fair in 1892, exhibits included culinary arts and embroidery displays, fossils, paintings, a number of barnyard animals, and a dog show. The *Billings Gazette* of October 5 reported "the dog show was well patronized, there being not less than thirty canines of all sorts and descriptions, big and little, barking and yelping at one and the same time."[10]

O'Donnell's grandson, Harley O'Donnell, who lives on the Hesper Farm property today, says his grandfather's willingness to diversify made him such an outstanding farmer. He had a multitude of interests and talents, all of which he used to good advantage for the Billings community—and the country. He was a good and conservative manager, always reminding people to "diversify" and "raise what you feed and feed what you raise."

Charlie Bair, who arrived in Billings in 1883 with only fourteen cents and five green apples, according to his biographer, Lee Rostad, made a fortune running thousands of sheep and making shrewd investments. Bair was a generous man who enjoyed providing outings and other treats for the crippled children at the St. Vincent Hospital-School. One of the nuns at the hospital-school said, "Celebrations of major holidays were among his specialties."[11] Bair eventually moved his family to a home he built in Martinsdale on the family ranch, although he maintained a room in the Northern Hotel for his frequent visits to Billings. His two daughters, Marguerite and Alberta, and Mrs. Bair made sure the ranch home had the finest furnishings available, including priceless china, silver, and art work, much

Billings Newspaper Men

1. E. H. Becker, formerly publisher of The Gazette. 2. C. Francis, Associated Press representative of The Daily Gazette. 3. Ralph Morris, business manager of The Times. 4. Theo. L. Stanton, publisher The Enquirer. 5. J. A. Gilluly, editor and business manager The Daily Journal. 6. M. C. Morris, editor The Times. 7. Judge J. D. Matheson, the veteran newspaper man of Billings, now retired. 8. R. G. Linebarger, editor The Daily Gazette. 9. E. P. Neill, city editor The Daily Journal. 10. Jean P. Decker, veteran newspaper man, now secretary Billings Chamber of Commerce. 11. Clifton Ham, business manager The Gazette Publishing Co. 12. E. W. Beedle, editor and proprietor The Yellowstone Monthly.

The growing community of Billings attracted a number of journalists and newspapers, as indicated by this picture of prominent newsmen of the day. THE *YELLOWSTONE MONTHLY*, DECEMBER 1907, BILLINGS CHAMBER OF COMMERCE

The *Billings Gazette* today. ROB MASSEE

of which was purchased on their trips to Europe. Upon Alberta's death, the house became a museum. The Bair Family Foundation continues to fund a number of educational, cultural, and community programs both in the Billings area and in Wheatland and Meagher counties.

The Yegen brothers, Christian and Peter, came to the United States from Switzerland and arrived in Billings in 1882. Their first business was a bakery; that was so successful that they branched out into selling groceries and then general merchandise. The Yegen Brothers Store was well known and catered to a clientele not only from Billings, but also from the surrounding territory. By 1900, they were able to open their own bank. One of their marketing techniques was painting a large Yegen Brothers sign on the side of Four Dances Cliff where it was visible for miles.

Albert L. Babcock opened his hardware store in "downtown" Billings in 1882, and like many of the other businessmen of that day, he diversified, serving also as president of the Yellowstone National Bank, the Yellowstone Fair Association, and the Billings Telephone Company. He also was elected twice to the state legislature. His name is still well known in Billings because the Babcock Theater he built to replace his Billings Opera House, which burned down in 1906, still draws crowds, once mainly for its Thursday night boxing matches, but now renovated and able to host a variety of events.

Paul McCormick, who was known as the "Grand Old Man of Montana," and John D. Losekamp also deserve mention. McCormick, who had been a freighter and an explorer in his younger years, owned the Seven Bar Seven Ranch, and built a lovely home in Billings, the scene of many gala events. Buffalo Bill Cody and Teddy Roosevelt were among his many guests. In fact, to accommodate the overflow of visitors to the McCormick home, he constructed a log guesthouse on his property. That log cabin was later moved to the top of the Rims to form part of the building that houses the Yellowstone County Museum. Losekamp was a Billings merchant who was a great supporter of education. He

Two influential early Billingsites, Paul McCormick and John Losekamp, for whom Losekamp Hall on the Rocky Mountain College campus is named, are shown here with a Billings Traction Trolley. In addition to the home that he built in the 1800s, McCormick constructed a large log guesthouse on his property. WESTERN HERITAGE CENTER

Paul McCormick's log "cabin" was eventually moved to the top of the Rimrocks, where it continues to welcome visitors to Billings as part of the Yellowstone County Museum. ROB MASSEE

contributed heavily to the establishment of the Billings Polytechnic Institute, which is now Rocky Mountain College. He died in 1913, and in 1919, a newly constructed building on the campus was named "Losekamp Hall" to honor his memory.

Although he cannot be counted among the most prominent of Billings businessmen, Parmly Billings, Frederick's youngest son, was the only Billings family member who lived in the community named for his father. He also took up a homestead nearby, but it didn't take long for him to decide that was not the life for him. Instead, he and his cousin, Edward Bailey, with some backing from the Billings family, opened the Bailey & Billings Bank.

The city of Billings was incorporated on April 3, 1885. The following day, Parmly wrote to his sister Mary. He shared his vision for the growing city, saying, "We intend to annex New York and there is some talk of hitching on Boston." And, he added, "I had some people come to me and ask your reprobate brother, exiled from home and friends, to let them use his name as a candidate for the office of mayor." He declined, "but I must tell you a 20 foot pole would not have touched me if I had been elected to that office. I would rather be mayor of the city of Billings than president of the U.S.A."[12]

Unfortunately, Parmly died of a sudden illness while traveling east to visit his parents in 1888. He was only twenty-five years old.

Some credit must also be given to the men who formed a volunteer fire department in the early years of the city's existence. The first such group was known as the Yellowstone Hook & Ladder Company; after a period of time, they disbanded for a while but came back as the Maverick Hose Company in 1889. The Maverick Hose Company fire bell hangs today in a place of honor on the Montana State University Billings campus, where it is rung on special occasions.

Among the more interesting women in Billings in its first two decades were Martha Jane Canary a.k.a. Calamity Jane and Olive "Ollie" Warren, a well-known madam and businesswoman. Stories abound about both women, and in *Billings A to Z*, Karen D. Stevens and Dee Ann Redman bring them together in one of Calamity's most talked-about escapades: "On one occasion, [Calamity] entered a Billings store with an axe and threatened to harm a clerk, and only the intervention of several men prevented her from doing so. Eyewitness B. R. Albin claimed the clerk was Olive Warren, who promptly quit and went into a different line of merchandising."[13]

Calamity Jane in a more familiar pose—rifle in one hand and the reins of her horse in the other. WESTERN HERITAGE CENTER

Whether that story is true or not, it is reflective of the frontier feel of Billings in its early years, when obviously some of the women were just as tough as the men. It certainly is true that Calamity took after a clerk in the Yegen Store with a hatchet, and whether or not the intended victim was Ollie Warren, later the proprietor of the Lucky Diamond "sporting house," it makes a good story. (When the more straight-laced citizens in town demanded the closure of the Lucky Diamond and other such establishments, Warren used the proceeds from the sale of her building to purchase both a Wyoming

The Yegen store with its wide range of goods drew a number of Crow Indians as customers. Their store was also the scene of a attempted hatchet attack when Calamity Jane burst in and chased a woman clerk around the store, threatening to kill her with the hatchet she was brandishing. Jane was a fairly frequent guest in the local jail or hospital, where she was diagnosed as "alcoholized." WESTERN HERITAGE CENTER

In the late 1890s, Minnesota Avenue was the picture of a frontier town with frame false-front buildings and appropriately garbed women on horseback. WESTERN HERITAGE CENTER

ranch and the Virginia Hotel on Montana Avenue; in the 1937 Billings City Directory, she was still listed as the "manager" of that establishment.)

And regardless of Calamity Jane's failings in terms of public morality and refined

In 1894, part of the Yellowstone County Fair was held at the corner of Minnesota Avenue and South Twenty-eighth Street. In addition to the interesting broom display, note the raised wooden sidewalk and the "streetlight" advertising the Blue Grass establishment to the right. WESTERN HERITAGE CENTER

or "ladylike" behavior, and her apparent disregard of established rules and/or laws, she did have a softer side and often provided needed services in Billings and elsewhere as a caring and competent, although untrained, nurse. In the absence of a hospital in early Billings, people in the community depended on the skills and willingness to care for the ill or injured of women like Jane and Mrs. Patrick O'Rourke and Mrs. Sarah Thompson, who cared for the county poor in their home.

There were many goodhearted and respectable souls in early Billings; in fact, they far outnumbered the criminal class in the community, although the latter often received the most press coverage. One example of how people looked out for one another will suffice to illustrate this. Agnes Soule was born during an Indian raid near Silver City, Idaho. She came to the Billings area as a young bride in 1889. Sadly, her first husband died after a horse fell on him and the doctor did not arrive in time to save him. She took her young daughter with her into Billings and checked into a hotel. Within hours, a local woman knocked on her door and invited her to stay at her home. "This is no place for a woman and child," she said. Agnes later married her benefactor's son and became a stalwart of the Billings chapters of the Daughters of the American Revolution and the Mayflower Descendents, as well as holding state offices in PEO.

CHANGING THE FACE OF THE RIMS

Any number of changes and alterations were to be expected when the Clark's Fork Bottom suddenly became home to a large number of settlers after centuries of being a sea bottom and then home to the indigenous tribes that roamed this territory. But it still came as a shock when Joseph Zimmerman, a rancher who lived west of Billings, sought a more time-efficient way to move his flock of more than two thousand sheep to summer pasture on the Rims. He had been taking them all the way along the base of the Rims to a spot east of Boot Hill Cemetery and then traveling back nearly the distance he had come to deliver them to their summer grazing area—certainly not the most efficient way to move animals their owner was trying to fatten up, especially since they had to return the same way in the fall. Zimmerman's brother Frank was put in charge of constructing a pathway up the Rims that would eliminate many miles from and shorten the time required to make the twice-yearly sheep drives. Thus was born Zimmerman Trail—a very rough trail when it was blasted out of the sandstone cliffs but now an important entrance and exit point in west Billings where it connects with Highway 3, which runs along the top of the Rims. Zimmerman Trail was recently extended through Billings proper to connect with the large commercial areas being developed in southwest Billings.

The Arcade building once housed a rather notorious bar but has been refurbished as a fast food restaurant and an office building by architect Randy Hafer, who has saved and restored several downtown buildings. ROB MASSEE

CHURCHES SPRING UP

Despite, or perhaps because of, the wilder side of early Billings, churches started appearing on streets that had once boasted only businesses and saloons. (Certainly the more family-oriented of the city's residents would have applauded this further sign of civilizing influences in a still rough-

The Union Train station, now used for social events, is located on Montana Avenue. ROB MASSEE

around-the-edges settlement.) The Reverend B. F. Shuart arrived in 1882—some say as an emissary for Frederick Billings to keep an eye on the progress of the town and report back—and organized the Congregational Church, Billings' first church. (The first church building was replaced the following year with a more permanent structure, funded by a donation from Frederick Billings, who was not a Congregationalist.) A Methodist Church and an Episcopal Church were also founded in 1882, and before the nineteenth century ended, a Baptist Church and an African Methodist Church were also holding services. In 1887, a Father Holton secured two lots at Second Avenue and North Thirty-first Street and built St. Joachim Catholic Church where visiting priests could say Mass. It would be ten years before there was a resident priest in Billings, but when Father Francis Van Clarenbeck arrived in the spring of 1897, Dr. Henry Chapple, who had come to Billings in 1889 with his brothers Dr. James and Charles, was mayor.

The first fair was held in 1894 at what is now the North Park area. WESTERN HERITAGE CENTER

Calamity Jane's cabin on Canyon Creek, west of Billings.
ARTHUR F. SALSBURY PHOTOGRAPH, BOB FEARS COLLECTION, WESTERN HERITAGE CENTER

Dr. Henry Chapple had long wanted to procure a hospital for his up-and-coming community, and the two men eventually decided that their best prospect for a hospital rested with the Sisters of Charity of Leavenworth, Kansas, who already had hospitals in western Montana. The two men traveled to Leavenworth to make their appeal, and the Sisters agreed to build a hospital in Billings.

It should come as no surprise that the building sites made available to the Sisters of Charity of Leavenworth for their hospital were offered by some prominent names in early Billings history, including the Yegen brothers and a group known as the Billings Real Estate and Development Company, which included P. B. Moss, H. W. Rowley, and I. D. O'Donnell. The BRE&DC site was eventually chosen, and within a few years, Moss, Rowley, and O'Donnell built family homes in the same neighborhood, now known as the Billings Historic District.

The first St. Vincent Hospital opened on February 1, 1899, and admitted its first patient the next day. Its small staff of sisters was responsible not only for nursing duties, but also for doing yard work on the property, maintaining a garden, raising chickens, and for daily housekeeping chores, such as scrubbing floors, cooking, and doing laundry.

As a positive way to cap the end of the 1890s, the Billings baseball team won the Northwest Championship title in 1899. According to Rick Underwood of the *Billings Gazette*, that team "rolled up some outrageous scores—42–2, 17–6, 36–3, and 26–15—while winning its first six games at home. They ended the year with a 17–5 mark. The final series of the year against Helena attracted a former senator, a former governor and a U.S. Marshal. The estimated attendance was 3,000."[14]

BILLINGS LIFE IN THE 1890S: AN ACCOUNT BY BEN STEELE SR.

One of the finest accounts of life in early Billings and the surrounding area can be found in "Some Memories of Billings and Eastern Montana" by Ben Steele Sr. This paper, which was delivered at a meeting of the Eastern Montana Pioneers on May 29, 1971, by noted artist Ben Steele Jr., was compiled and written by Shirley Steele, a well-known poet, who interviewed her father-in-law to capture his memories of early Billings.

Steele Sr. begins his reminiscence with his arrival in Billings in March of 1890, when he was nine years old. "We had come by train to Butte and by bobsled to Jefferson Island (now Cardwell) where my mother's uncle, Senator Cardwell, lived. We boarded the train for Billings in Logan. . . . In the East I had heard a lot about cowpunchers—that they were a pretty rough bunch.

"When I started to ride to school in Billings [from the Ed Cardwell ranch west of town], there was only one house on Grand Avenue between our place and town. Grand Avenue was known as Brick Yard Road then, and the house was of stone and built by Jack Partington in the 1880s. Jack was a stonemason who owned the land where West Park Plaza now stands. . . .

"In 1893 when my sister Mae started to school, we drove in a two-wheel cart. The only school was located between 29th and 30th Street North on 4th Avenue. There was a big slough north of the school on 6th Avenue where we used to skate during recess and at noon. Another big bog hole covered most of the flat occupied by Alderson, Burlington, and Lewis Avenues. But when the drain ditches were dug, these dried up and were filled in. Then we skated on Clanton Lake, situated about 200 yards west of Clanton's house, which was on top of the hill north of the present site of Billings Senior High School.

A cable ferry, perhaps similar to the one operated by Thomas McGirl. WESTERN HERITAGE CENTER

"Billings was truly a small town in the 1890s. There were no bridges across the Yellowstone—only ferries. There was a ferry to Blue Creek south of town and one north of the railroad bridge east of town. How I loved to cross on the ferries. Our family and friends made several trips every fall to Pryor Creek to hunt prairie chickens and gather wild plums and chokecherries. All were plentiful.

"In the early 1890s, the Yegen Brothers ran the only grocery store in town where Elliot's furniture store is now. Later Donovan and Spear started a grocery store. Then Spear sold his interest to McCormack and it became Donovan and McCormack. Pete Smith had the only livery stable for a time. It was located north of Wagner's clothing store. Jack Bond was the blacksmith with a shop next door to the livery stable. Then Jeff Brewer opened The Dark Horse Livery Barn, and Gib Cothren and John Todd started the Cothren and Todd Barn where Hart-Albin's stands now [in 2009 the site of Montana State University Billings Downtown]. Joe Zimmerman and John D. Losekamp owned the only clothing stores at that time.

"Mr. Losekamp was one of the best-loved men in the community. Every Christmas he handed out treats to all the children. Cowboys who hadn't had a winter job and were broke in the spring knew he would stake them to a tarpaulin, blankets, sugar, and clothing for a fresh start. And as soon as they earned the money they came in and paid him every cent they owed. He told me he never lost a nickel on them. Mr. Losekamp also put up money to start the polytechnic school, now Rocky Mountain College, and left an inheritance to the school when he passed away.

"A streetcar connected Billings with Coulson in the early nineties. Twenty-five cents bought a ride to Coulson and a glass of beer when you got there. Frank Mann ran the saloon out there. But in spite of the hospitality, old Coulson gradually died. Some of the buildings were moved to Billings and the rest disappeared in time. Frank Mann became police judge in Billings and was known as Judge Mann.

"Many a Billings citizen had a cow barn and a chicken house at the back of his lot. Pat Rorick ran the town cowherd for a number of years. He would [collect the cows from their owners and] take them to a pasture out in the west end of town in the morning and fetch them back at night.

"They hanged a man here in Billings in the early nineties. It happened that two bums came into town, went in to Joe Clancy's saloon, ordered some beer, and wouldn't pay for it. When Joe ordered them out, one of them picked up a beer mallet and beat Joe to death. Well, they were captured and thrown in jail, but that night a group of citizens went to the jail and ordered Sheriff John Ramsey to turn the murderer over to them. He refused, so the vigilante group took a battering ram and broke down the door. They took the murderer and hanged him on a telegraph pole about where the depot is today. He wasn't cut down until eleven o'clock the next day. The other bum was turned loose, and the last anyone saw of him he was headed across the railroad bridge east of town on a high run. When father and I came in to town that morning, the first things we heard about were the murder and the hanging. We went to see the man. He was the only man I ever saw after he was hanged. . . .

"Sam Salsbury drove a dray wagon in Billings for years. A fine sorrel team pulled the dray. I can see him yet, standing on the dray; he would crack that long whip of his and away he would go! . . .

"A Chinaman grew vegetables on a small farm where Division Street and Grand Avenue come together. He lived in a one-room log cabin and sold his vegetables around town, peddling them from baskets suspended at each end of a long pole balanced on his back. Albert Clanton and I passed this farm every day on our way to school.

"Calamity Jane was seen often in and around Billings at the turn of the century. Near her cabin on Canyon Creek was a hill where she and her gang hid stolen horses. The top of the hill could be reached only from the southwest corner. When the gang had gathered a bunch of horses, they drove them out of the country and sold them. Calamity Jane always dressed like a man and could out-swear and out-drink any man around . . . .

"One of the first settlers in the Billings area was O. N. Newman. He came in the eighties and raised a large family of 8 boys and 2 girls. The first school in the area was erected on his ranch and still [in 1971] stands. Mr. Newman ran a dairy and for many years supplied Coulson and Billings with milk. All the Newman boys liked to hunt and supplied the family with meat. There were no limits; you could kill as many as you could use. . . .

"In 1894 a group of men attempting to join Coxey's Army came through Billings on a train they had stolen in Butte. I hurried to the depot with four other kids to see the excitement. Some U.S. Marshals were there from Helena to arrest the men. The marshals ordered the men to surrender, but a group of Billings citizens grabbed the marshals' guns, broke them over the railroad tracks, and chased the marshals back to their car. Several shots were fired and one man was killed. We kids hid behind a boxcar until the shooting stopped. Mike Flanigan presented the army boys with a big red rooster, and when the train pulled out, one of them stood on the back platform waving the rooster. The Montana contingent never made it to Washington, however, because the governor called out the militia, which stopped the 'Army' at Miles City and returned the train to Butte."[15]

Ed Cardwell was a cousin of Ben Steele Senior's mother, and father of Zella Cardwell who married Peter Yegen Jr.

The nineteenth century drew to a close with optimism over the future of Billings high and the little community that had begun life just a few years earlier as a town of tents and hastily constructed wooden shacks looking forward to continued growth and prosperity in the new century.

Window shoppers discuss the offerings at the Lee & McNaught shop while a bicyclist stops in front of the Billings Bookbindery and the Billings Electric Supply Company in the 2800 block of First Avenue North. A Crow woman and her child rest in the shade of the buildings. ARTHUR F. SALSBURY PHOTOGRAPH, BOB FEARS COLLECTION, WESTERN HERITAGE CENTER

Chapter TWO
BILLINGS IN THE EARLY TWENTIETH CENTURY,
1900–1920

DESTINATION: BILLINGS, MONTANA

Those optimistic pioneers who moved to Billings because they saw the promise of a prosperous future in a growing community were not disappointed. Between 1899 and 1909, the population of Billings grew by 211.4 percent. Only five other places in the United States had a higher growth rate in that time period.[1]

As befitted a growing community, a number of new businesses and buildings were springing up, not in tents as when the city was in its infancy, but in the substantial brick and sandstone structures a community assured of a future would construct.

The Parmly Billings Memorial Library was a gift to the city by Frederick Billings Jr. as a memorial to his brother who had died at twenty-five of a sudden illness. Parmly Billings was the only member of the Billings family who actually lived in the town named for his father. WESTERN HERITAGE CENTER

Frederick Billings Jr. donated the Parmly Billings Memorial Library to the city in memory of his younger brother. This impressive building, now the Western Heritage Center, was dedicated in October of 1901. In December of the same year, Rocky Mountain Bell Telephone Company opened an exchange allowing Billings customers to place long distance calls to several Montana towns as far away as Butte. The Hart Albin store opened in January of 1902 and sold almost $60 worth of goods in its first day of operation. By 1903, the Billings City Hall was completed, and plans were in the works for a permanent jail. (Unfortunately, as the town grew in its early years, it apparently attracted almost as many ne'er-do-wells as respectable, churchgoing family types. During its first decade in operation, St. Vincent Hospital, in addition to caring for patients struggling with typhoid and tuberculosis, also saw numerous cases of broken jaws and cut and bruised faces, suggesting that brawls of minor or major proportions were a frequent occurrence.)

Several prominent families built impressive homes shortly after the turn of the century. As noted earlier, three of these homes were in the vicinity of the first St. Vincent Hospital at Division Street and Broadwater Avenue, where Billings Catholic Central High School now stands.

The P. B. Moss family home was constructed from 1901 to 1903. This twenty-eight-room red sandstone structure was designed by H. J. Hardenberg, a well-known New York architect, and built by local contractor E. H. Gagnon. It was home to the Moss family, which included six children, Mrs. Moss's parents, and the household staff. (Their groundskeeper had a room in the barn at the back of the property.)

Hart Albin was Billings' premier store from 1902 to 1990, when the company went out of business. Dr. Harriet Foxton Clark, Billings' first female physician, and her husband, Dr. Andrew Clark, had offices on the second floor of the Hart Albin building. WESTERN HERITAGE CENTER

The Hart Albin building, on the corner of Second Avenue North and North Twenty-eighth Street, is currently occupied by D. A. Davidson and Montana State University Billings' downtown campus. KEVIN KOOISTRA-MANNING

The I. D. O'Donnell home, listed on the National Register of Historic Places, remains a family residence. ROB MASSEE

The Henry Rowley home on Clark Avenue was built in the early 1900s. ROB MASSEE

An associate of Moss in the sheep business, T. A. Snidow, built a more modest but still impressive brick home, just across Yellowstone Avenue to the south of the Moss home, during this same period, and I. D. O'Donnell moved his family into their Victorian-style home, graced by a three-story octagonal turret and bay windows, on January 1, 1905. The O'Donnell home, at 105 Clark Avenue, was also close to the Moss home. H. W. Rowley's family home, across Clark Avenue from the O'Donnell residence, had a brick "fence," designed to keep wandering livestock out of the yard.

Real estate developer Austin North chose to build his impressive home, known locally as "The Castle," in the hinterlands of Billings in 1902–03. While Moss, Snidow, Rowley, and O'Donnell built on what was then the western edge of the city, North chose a far northeast

Austin North, Billings entrepreneur, seen here in his real estate office, built his palatial home—known as "The Castle"—in the early 1900s. WESTERN HERITAGE CENTER

"The Castle" as it appears today. The turn-of-the-twentieth-century building now serves as office and living space for owner Corby Skinner ("Mr. Billings"). KEVIN KOOISTRA-MANNING

The original Smith's mortuary on Second Avenue North was also home to an ambulance service. In 2007, the structure was razed for the construction of a city parking garage, and the mortuary business moved into the former Bungalow restaurant on South Twenty-seventh Street. WESTERN HERITAGE CENTER

location for his three-story brick home, reportedly modeled after an English castle. (Because North was a prominent businessman, many people believe that North Park was named for him, but that is not the case. North Park, the site of the first fairgrounds, and South Park were both named for their locations in the community.)

Architects and builders were kept busy during the early 1900s with homes and other building projects, such as Moss and Rowley's Northern Hotel, under construction. The Magic City was living up to its early promise, and the graceful design of the Northern Hotel spoke to the importance of this growing city—and of the people who would be drawn to it, either as permanent residents or as noteworthy visitors.

G. Herman Smith, founder of Smith Funeral Home, expanded his services in 1904 to include an ambulance service. The downtown building that housed both businesses stood until 2007 when it was razed to provide more parking in the downtown area.

In 1905, construction began on St. Patrick's Church, now designated as a co-cathedral of the Great Falls-Billings Diocese of the Catholic Church in Montana. The church was dedicated in 1906 with ceremonies commencing at 10:00 a.m. and continuing through the day and into the evening. The church was estimated to have cost close to $100,000. (In 2000, the original building was remodeled, and in 2007 the original rectory, next to the church, was replaced with a parish center.)

And, of course, homes and business buildings on a more modest scale continued to be built in neighborhoods radiating out in all directions from the busy hub of the downtown business district.

Sheriff James T. Webb, Billings, circa 1905. WESTERN HERITAGE CENTER

BILLINGS MOURNS ITS SHERIFF

On Tuesday, March 24, 1908, Sheriff James Webb was attempting to apprehend William Bickford, a horse thief, on a ranch near Roundup when Bickford emerged from a wagon where he had been dressing with a rifle in his hands. Before the sheriff could pull his own gun, Bickford had shot him dead and fled the scene.

Outraged citizens showed up at the courthouse as word spread about the death of the popular sheriff and "scores of men offered their services to the undersheriff and all were eager to start out after the murderer of Webb," according to the Billings Daily Journal of March 25. "Rifles were hastily procured and placed in the hands of men who could be depended upon to use them as the occasion demanded. Automobiles, horses, and other means of conveyance were quickly brought into requisition, and the chase for Bickford began in earnest."[2]

Sheriff James Webb, killed in the line of duty when he tried to arrest a horse thief, is remembered by a drinking fountain on the courthouse lawn and by the Alex Mavity memorial plaque, which recognizes all the Billings lawmen lost in the city's history. KEVIN KOOISTRA-MANNING

Despite the rough terrain in the area where Bickford made his escape, he had no chance of outwitting or outrunning the posse that had been assembled, and he was, in fact, buried the same day that Sheriff Webb was laid to rest in the Billings Cemetery (now part of Mountview Cemetery) after a funeral service attended by "thousands of citizens, irrespective of creed or political affiliations, attesting

Helena Drake walks her dog near McKinley School, built by early-day architect John G. Link. McKinley was the dominant building on the northern edge of Billings in 1912. WESTERN HERITAGE CENTER

to the love and esteem in which the brave officer was held by all. The crowd was so great that many were unable to gain admittance, and had the hall been twice as large it would not have accommodated the entire assemblage," according to the *Billings Daily Journal* evening edition on the day of the funeral. The *Journal* even ran a poetic tribute by a poet who chose to sign his or her work only with the initials C. A. R.: "To feel that he, by traitor's hand, was stricken;/To know the faithful form in death lies low,/The active brain no more in life will quicken;/Now makes us with a silent grief bow low."[3]

Billings' schoolchildren collected pennies to fund a memorial to the fallen sheriff. The Webb Memorial Drinking Fountain, no longer in use, was constructed on land adjacent to the courthouse.

FIRST PERSON ACCOUNTS

Although Billings was becoming more and more "citified" in terms of family neighborhoods, business opportunities, stores, services, churches, parks, cultural events, schools, etc., it still had many reminders of its rough beginnings and Western heritage. In 1911, a young Dale Eunson and his mother had come to Billings from their Acton-area homestead to do some shopping. As they walked east on Montana Avenue to the Hart Albin store, they "ran into a thousand sheep being driven to the stockyards for shipment to Chicago, and had to climb the [Parmly Billings Memorial] library steps to get out of their way."[4]

CHAPTER TWO BILLINGS IN THE EARLY TWENTIETH CENTURY, 1900–1920

Early Billings residents got around their growing community in a number of ways: on foot, on horseback, on bicycles, on trolleys, and in early automobiles. WESTERN HERITAGE CENTER

Soon after 1912, family homes sprung up in the vicinity of the McKinley School. ROB MASSEE

Still, the Billings the Eunson mother and son visited was an up-and-coming city, with a population by 1910 of more than ten thousand—and enough traffic that the *Billings Gazette* was urging the city fathers to adopt a federal speed limit to regulate drivers who sped through town—unless they were halted by livestock on the road, of course.

Eunson was not the only budding writer living in or near Billings in the early decades of the twentieth century. Louis Lundborg, who went on to become the chairman of the Bank of America, recorded his memories in *Up to Now*: "Billings in the 1910s was as nearly a classless society as anyone could envision. There were families with more money and families with less, but no one could see any line between the two.

"We all attended the same schools; and not only did we all play on the same football teams, act in the same plays, and belong to the same debating societies—but after school we went to each other's homes with no thought of 'crossing lines.'"[5]

35

Muddy in wet weather, dusty in dry, streets in Billings were originally "improved" by laying bricks or wood blocks on top of the soil. WESTERN HERITAGE CENTER

Gwendolen Haste, who arrived in Billings as a young woman in 1915, made a similar observation in her unpublished memoir, "Pattern of Time." Because her father had been brought to Billings by P. B. Moss to edit *The Scientific Farmer*, a publication Moss had purchased to publicize a new venture, the building of Mossmain, a planned city, several miles to the west of Billings, Gwenna, as she was called, became a close friend of the two oldest Moss daughters, Kula and Melville, and was a frequent visitor at the Moss home.

Haste recalled that during World War I, Mrs. Moss opened her home to all the women of Billings to roll bandages and/or to knit socks, caps, and gloves for soldiers. And if a woman didn't know how to knit or how to roll bandages, she was welcome to come and learn those skills.

Lundborg told of the recreational activities available to the youngsters of Billings in the second decade of the twentieth century, including sliding down the cellar doors of the town's first courthouse and ice skating, either on a frozen Alkali Creek or at the town's skating rink, which moved from one location to another, depending on where the best open field might be found.

The man in charge of the winter skating program seemed an unlikely choice—old "Packsaddle Ben" Greenough, a former "mountain man" (and friend and business partner of Calamity Jane).

CHAPTER TWO BILLINGS IN THE EARLY TWENTIETH CENTURY, 1900–1920

Despite the perils of muddy, dusty, and bumpy roads, some progressive early Billingsites got around town in their automobiles. R. L. Baker, an early automobile dealer, and his wife are seen cruising on North Thirty-first in about 1912. Today, there are at least fifteen new car dealerships in the city, many used-car lots, and a dozen or more other dealerships just a few miles away in any direction. ARTHUR F. SALSBURY PHOTOGRAPH, BOB FEARS COLLECTION, WESTERN HERITAGE CENTER

The original depot on North Broadway (North Twenty-eighth Street) blocked access across the railroad tracks. When a new depot was built in 1907, Broadway was opened to connect with its southern cousin on the other side of the tracks. WESTERN HERITAGE CENTER

Greenough would search out the best spot, supervise the flooding of the field, and teach the children who hadn't skated before how to negotiate the slippery surface on new skates—or simply blades strapped to everyday shoes.

In the summer months, swimming was the sport of choice, and for the youngsters, skinny dipping in the Big Ditch was the favorite way to cool off, even though parents and city officials warned them against it. (Probably safety was a greater concern than modesty; the Big Ditch has taken many lives through the years.) Nonetheless, the lure (and adventure) was too much to resist, and Lundborg recounts, "We usually swam far enough from the Twenty-seventh Street Bridge so that modesty was no problem; but part of the fun was diving from that same bridge. If we made it to the bridge without being seen, we could climb up and dive from the railing; but half the time we would have to dive from the ditch bank to hide from . . . the occasional buggy that drove by."[6]

The Billings all three of these writers recalled was indeed a bustling community, growing almost daily, with new people, new enterprises, and new entertainment possibilities coming and going on the twenty east- and westbound Burlington and Northern Pacific trains arriving and departing daily at the Union Station. The Magic City was truly living up to its affectionate nickname.

The December 27, 1911, supplement of the *Weekly Bulletin* featured a progress report on Billings, which it called the "Gateway to the Northwest," praising its climate ("most delightful") and naming it "undoubtedly Montana's most promising city." Its "excellent educational facilities" included "nine public school buildings and an accredited high school, a parochial school, a commercial college, a night school and a polytechnic college which gives industrial and collegiate courses." According to the *Bulletin*, 2,200 students were attending classes in the city's schools offered by seventy teachers, "either college or normal [school] trained."[7]

Billings L. and I. Co's. Ditch and Flume Billings, Mont.

This early postcard shows a ditch and flume across Alkali Creek, originally operated by the Billings Land and Irrigation Company and now owned by the Billings Bench Water Association. WESTERN HERITAGE CENTER

Of equal importance were the "16 church organizations in Billings, ten of which have their own church edifices and three others of which have purchased ground on which to build." The churches represented in this tally included "Methodist, Congregationalist, Presbyterian, Christian, Episcopalian, Baptist, Adventist, Church of Christ, Spiritualist, African, Lutheran and some minor sects."[8] There was a Jewish community in Billings, but it would not organize until mid-century.

The *Bulletin* even reported "34 secret and fraternal societies." While it seems strange that one could get an exact count of "secret societies," it is obvious that a good many of these "fraternal" organizations were, indeed, the province of the men in the community. "The Masonic organizations have a handsome new temple costing $115,000; the Elks have a club house costing $135,000, not including about $50,000 worth of gifts [presumably furnishings and the like]; the Odd Fellows have a hall costing about $50,000, and the Eagles have purchased ground for a building in the business district which will be erected in the near future."[9] Such organizations would continue to be an important part of the community until the end of the century when many fraternal groups, even those that had admitted women to their ranks, saw declining memberships.

After beginning life with a number of newspapers, by 1911 Billings, continuing that tradition, had, in addition to the *Weekly Bulletin*, "two daily, one semiweekly, two weekly and three monthly papers to 'cover the field.' The dailies are the *Gazette*, morning, with full Associated Press reports, and the *Journal*, evening, with United and Associated Press service."[10]

CHAPTER TWO BILLINGS IN THE EARLY TWENTIETH CENTURY, 1900–1920

Eaton Hall at Rocky Mountain College. Eaton Hall is named for the founders of Billings Polytechnic Institute, Lewis T. and Ernest T. Eaton. ROB MASSEE

The steps, east of North Twenty-seventh Street, are no longer in general use and are not safe for all but the most skilled climbers—and maybe not even them. Most visitors to the top of the Rims now arrive by car. TABATHA ELSBERRY

Entertainment could be enjoyed at "the finest theater between Chicago and the Pacific coast," the Babcock, which could seat 1,300, and at "three vaudeville and four motion picture theaters, playing the Fisher, Webster and Sullivan and Considine circuit attractions."[11]

Billings also had "excellent mail facilities," according to the *Bulletin*, with a "first class" post office, which employed "fourteen clerks and six city carriers."[12]

And the city had "cause to be proud of its public buildings, including the Yellowstone County Courthouse and a white pressed brick City Hall." Plans were underway for a federal building, and "the Sisters hospital is a fine structure built of pressed brick and modernly equipped." To keep all these structures safe, "Billings has a paid [fire] department, occupying two two-story brick structures . . . The equipment is the best and includes an automobile engine and hose wagon."[13]

Despite the fine and well-equipped fire department, Peter Yegen's store, which was well stocked with ammunition and powder kegs, could not be saved when a fire started in September of 1909 in the basement and was helped along by exploding combustibles. Firemen did manage to confine the damage to the one store, however. And they had better luck the following year when firemen, who had been fighting another fire, saw flames coming from the chimney of the Northern Hotel and managed to put out a fire in the furnace room, thus giving that beautiful structure another thirty years of gracing downtown Billings.

The second decade of the twentieth century in Billings saw growth and change, certainly, with the city reaching a population of more than twenty thousand by 1919. It also saw its share of turmoil and trouble, beginning with a polio pandemic in 1916 and the United States entry into World War I the following year, followed by the influenza epidemic of 1918–19 which claimed so many lives across the country.

Early Billings residents made frequent use of bicycles to travel around town. WESTERN HERITAGE CENTER

In July of 1916, polio arrived in Billings and nearly overwhelmed the already shorthanded medical personnel in the community. (Although the United States had not yet entered the war, troop buildups had taken several physicians and other health providers away from their home communities, and Billings was no exception.) Dr. Louis Allard, a Laurel native who opened a practice in Billings in 1914, asked St. Vincent Hospital officials to designate one ward as a polio unit, and he and Sister Arcadia Lea, SCL, began a treatment program that brought hundreds of victims of that disease—and other crippling conditions—to Billings. "Uncle Louie," as Allard was affectionately known to the hospital staff, and Sister Arcadia became known as "Miracle Workers" to people throughout the area, and before long, the original St. Vincent Hospital was so crowded with orthopedic patients that an "annex" had to be opened in a building across the street. (In 1923, when the "new" St. Vincent Hospital

CHAPTER TWO BILLINGS IN THE EARLY TWENTIETH CENTURY, 1900–1920

Montana Avenue and North Broadway in 1902. Note the Chapple Drugstore to the right and the telephone lines to the left. Billings had early phone service. The Parmly Billings Library is on the far left. This picture must have been taken early on a Sunday morning, given the lack of traffic, foot or vehicle. WESTERN HERITAGE CENTER

A parade of motorists celebrates the opening of Polytechnic Drive. The Billings Polytechnic Institute campus can be seen in the background in this 1920 view. Students constructed the buildings from sandstone quarried from the Rimrocks in the background. ROCKY MOUNTAIN COLLEGE PHOTOGRAPH, WESTERN HERITAGE CENTER

In 1914, Dr. Frank Bell made history when he flew from Billings to Park City, twenty-five miles away, and back.
JENSEN COLLECTION, WESTERN HERITAGE CENTER

Dr. Frank Bell attempts a takeoff at the original Billings fairgrounds, where North Park is now located, on Memorial Day, 1913. ARTHUR F. SALSBURY PHOTOGRAPH, BOB FEARS COLLECTION, WESTERN HERITAGE CENTER

opened, the original hospital building became a "Hospital School," where youngsters undergoing long confinements could be educated by a small staff of volunteer teachers.)

The war years took a toll on Billings as they did across the country, not only in scarcity of certain items, but also in worry about the wellbeing of those who were serving. Even Gwendolen Haste, who recorded in "Pattern of Time" that "no one who had my heart went to war," says that after seeing a co-worker off to report for duty, she "burst into tears at the lunch table."[14]

Troop trains frequently came through Billings, and "canteens" were set up in the depot to serve food to traveling servicemen. There were also dances held where young ladies of the community entertained the soldiers—well chaperoned, of course. (Still, some romances were sparked, according to Billings old-timers.)

Once the war was over, it seemed a time for rejoicing and returning to normal peacetime pastimes, but in the winter of 1918–19, influenza struck Billings, and struck hard. So many people were so ill that the high school building became an auxiliary hospital. All the medical personnel in Billings were called in to help—including the school Sisters who took over nursing duties at the hospital

CHAPTER TWO BILLINGS IN THE EARLY TWENTIETH CENTURY, 1900–1920

This party of picnickers on the Rims reached their destination by taking the steps carved into the sandstone cliffs by Heffner Stone Quarry employees. The quarry was located at the base of the Rims to the north of the Montana State University Billings main campus.
WESTERN HERITAGE CENTER

By 1908, the Yellowstone County Fair had changed its name to the Midland Empire Fair and greatly expanded its offerings, as seen by this photo from the 1930s.
WESTERN HERITAGE CENTER

Fence straddlers and ground standers watch Bell fly overhead. Note the horse-drawn buggy to the right of the fence. The first automobile in Billings arrived in 1905; only eight years later, residents who were amazed by "horseless carriages" had another cause for disbelief—a man piloting a winged carriage in the sky overhead. ARTHUR F. SALSBURY PHOTOGRAPH, BOB FEARS COLLECTION, WESTERN HERITAGE CENTER

proper while the actual nursing Sisters worked alongside doctors, dentists, and nursing students (the hospital had started a school of nursing in 1913) at the high school. Community volunteers delivered meals to patients to free medical personnel for the more important task of treating the ill. Even Dr. Allard came down with a serious case of flu; for three days, he was delirious, but he finally regained consciousness, although he remained hospitalized for quite a while. And eventually, the city recovered from the ravages of the flu epidemic as well, but there were some other serious setbacks on the horizon for the region.

The Broadway side of the original Northern Hotel was decked out for a parade—and some lucky people had very comfortable viewing sites. Note the "Suburban Homes" awning to the left. Obviously, Billings was growing. ARTHUR F. SALSBURY PHOTOGRAPH, BOB FEARS COLLECTION, WESTERN HERITAGE CENTER

Billings served as a supply depot, medical center, and cultural center for a large area flooded with homesteaders after the 1909 passage of the Enlarged Homestead Act, which doubled the number of acres a homesteader could claim from 160 to 320 acres. (Most Montana counties more than doubled their population during these "boom years" for homesteading.) The promise of prosperity rising from the land in the form of abundant crops held during what Gwendolen Haste described as "the good years—the wet years—when every man who had taken the Great Northern bait was hopeful that hard work would get him his heart's desire, while the old-timers held their breath."[15]

A number of Crow, including Chief Plenty Coups, fourth from right, at the fairgrounds in the late 1920s. In the early years of the fair, members of the Crow tribe took part in large numbers, competing in horse and foot races, dancing contests, and other events. ARTHUR F. SALSBURY PHOTOGRAPH, BOB FEARS COLLECTION, WESTERN HERITAGE CENTER

CHAPTER TWO BILLINGS IN THE EARLY TWENTIETH CENTURY, 1900–1920

Zimmerman Trail before it was improved and paved. ARTHUR F. SALSBURY PHOTOGRAPH, BOB FEARS COLLECTION, WESTERN HERITAGE CENTER

Those old-timers didn't have long to wait. Haste wrote of "failing banks, heartsick farmers, limping businesses, and all the melancholy results of drought and disaster. Come 1917 the drouth began, reaching its climax in 1919, and precipitating a dreary depression when shacks were deserted, implements were retrieved by dealers or rusted in the fields, and small-town bankers shot themselves."[16]

Billings was not immune to the economic woes of the rest of the state, of course. People in this community who had catered to the needs of outlying regions—and profited in the process—also heard "the wind . . . of failure keening in their ears."[17]

Crow Chief Plenty Coups makes an appearance in Billings. ARTHUR F. SALSBURY PHOTOGRAPH, BOB FEARS COLLECTION, WESTERN HERITAGE CENTER

A familiar image of Calamity Jane with gun in hand and dressed more like a man than a woman. This was an image she sold to tourists as souvenirs of their visit to the still Wild West. WESTERN HERITAGE CENTER

Chapter THREE
BILLINGS IN THE 1920S AND '30S

DESTINATION MONTANA

Perhaps the most hopeful sign for Billings residents in the early 1920s when those "winds of failure" were beginning to keen was the idea of Billings as "The Oil Center" of the region. A graphic depiction of Billings drawn by E. L. H. Cummings in 1921 illustrates the distances to nearby oil fields by giving the hours taken to reach them by auto. Devil's Basin and Soap Creek were only two and one-half hours away; Elk Basin (which opened in 1915 as Montana's first oil field) was three and one-half hours; and Cat Creek, five and one-half hours.[1] Discoveries of oil and natural gas, as well as the coal deposits in the region, would continue to play a role in the evolving economic importance of Billings, as three refineries would be built in or near the city in the coming years.

The new St. Vincent Hospital opened on November 7, 1923, replacing the first hospital, which was converted into a hospital school to treat and educate crippled children, many of them victims of the polio pandemic that reached Billings in 1916. WESTERN HERITAGE CENTER

St. Vincent Healthcare, 2007. ROB MASSEE

And there was still work to be had in a community continuing to grow. After World War I, for example, when building materials were no longer needed for the war effort, construction began in earnest on some major projects, including the new St. Vincent Hospital on North Thirtieth Street and Twelfth Avenue North—the northern edge of town—which opened in 1923, and Deaconess Hospital, just a few blocks to the south, which welcomed its first patients in 1927. New homes were also springing up, and the state gave Billings a boost in 1925 when it selected it as the site for a new Normal School to serve the eastern part of the state.

A prime mover in the push for a unit of the University System in eastern Montana was the Billings Midland Club, incorporated in 1918, in part to bring a teachers' college to a region of the state previously underserved by the state's four higher education units, all of which were located in western Montana. Members of the Midland Club recognized that many returning veterans of World War I had their sights set on better opportunities than returning to the family farm, but they wanted to remain in Montana. The opportunity for further education seemed to be at least one avenue to making that happen.

The Billings Commercial Club, a forerunner of the Chamber of Commerce, raised the funds necessary to purchase land for the new campus and deeded the site to the state. The spot chosen was at

CHAPTER THREE BILLINGS IN THE 1920s AND '30s

The second hospital in Billings, Deaconess, now the Billings Clinic, under construction in 1926. It opened to receive patients on June 30, 1927.
WESTERN HERITAGE CENTER

the end of North Thirtieth, where it intersected with Poly Drive, named after the Polytechnic campus just a stone's throw to the west. The new St. Vincent Hospital was the most prominent structure in the area and only one long block from the future campus. By this time, Billings was an ever-growing community of twenty thousand people, which meant there would be rooms available in residential neighborhoods for out-of-town students to rent and several facilities where classes could be conducted until an actual campus could be built. Early classes were held all over Billings—in schools, at the YMCA, in warehouses—and Normal School students got a lot of exercise walking to and from their classrooms. (A Normal School was a teacher-training institution, called "Normal" because it instructed future teachers on how to present the "normal" subjects of reading, writing, and arithmetic. Students at the Eastern Montana Normal School also received instruction in music, drama, science, and physical education, fields very dear to the school's first president, Dr. Lynn McMullen.)

The Normal School students did their share to lift the gloom of the hard times in Montana by presenting plays and musical evenings for the community's enjoyment.

After the branding at the Rehberg Roundup, folks relaxed with a cool drink and lunch. Locals were invited to participate in the roundup and branding at the ranch, located west of Billings, in the vicinity of what is now Poly Drive and Rehberg Lane. ELTON SCHEIDECKER PHOTOGRAPH, WESTERN HERITAGE CENTER

49

THE KKK COMES TO BILLINGS

Not all the new arrivals in Billings in the 1920s were as welcome as the Normal School staff and students. For some reason, a number of Ku Klux Klansmen moved into the community and set about gathering new members. They even advertised in the *Gazette*, inviting queries from interested parties.

On one occasion, the Klan burned a cross on the Rims, which caused a power outage in the city. A surgery underway at St. Vincent Hospital had to be finished with emergency lighting, at risk to the patient. When the Sister administrator of the hospital met with the mayor the next day, she impressed upon him how serious the consequences could have been for the patient on the operating table and pointed out the mayor's duty to keep his fellow townsfolk safe. No more crosses were burned in Billings, and by the 1930s, Klan activity in this part of the state had pretty much ceased, although it continued elsewhere in Montana. (A brief resurgence of attempts to reintroduce the Klan to Billings in the 1990s led to some unfortunate incidents, but there was not enough interest—in fact, just the opposite—to keep the would-be organizers around for long.)

A JOYOUS CELEBRATION AS BILLINGS TURNS FORTY-FIVE

In 1927, Billings turned forty-five, and despite hard times across the state, the city was ready to celebrate in grand style. In March, the county commissioners approved a plan for a "scenic road" on top of the Rims, and at the end of that month, the park commission was ready to begin construction on the road, fulfilling a desire of the Commercial Club for such a byway as a tourist attraction.

William S. Hart (in the dark suit) was difficult to recognize without his Western garb and cowboy hat when he took part in a groundbreaking ceremony at the First Congregational Church. The little boy in white is Dewey Hansen, Billings native and longtime teacher at Billings Senior High School. ARTHUR F. SALSBURY PHOTOGRAPH, BOB FEARS COLLECTION, WESTERN HERITAGE CENTER

The new Deaconess Hospital opened on July 3, 1927, with tours for the public and accolades from the *Gazette*, which proclaimed in a subhead, "$250,000 Institution Gift From People of Midland Empire to Those Who Suffer." The new hospital had sixty-seven patient rooms and a central heating plant, and was certainly a reason for the citizens of Billings to feel they were living in a very progressive community.

Not surprisingly, the major celebrations of the anniversary were held on the Fourth of July. "[A] crowded program of pageantry, races, rodeo events and patriotic exercises . . . was held before an immense crowd, numbering 10,500 persons, at the Midland Fairgrounds" to celebrate both the Fourth and the forty-fifth anniversary, according to the *Gazette*.[2]

"The first part of the program was devoted to a historical spectacle which gave a panorama of the whole history of the frontier west; Crows

CHAPTER THREE BILLINGS IN THE 1920s AND '30s

The *Range Rider* gazes across Billings from its earlier location on the Black Otter Trail in 1930. ARTHUR F. SALSBURY PHOTOGRAPH, BOB FEARS COLLECTION, WESTERN HERITAGE CENTER

William S. Hart addresses the crowd at the dedication of the *Range Rider of the Yellowstone* statue. Charlie Bair is seated second from left on the improvised platform. ARTHUR F. SALSBURY PHOTOGRAPH, BOB FEARS COLLECTION, WESTERN HERITAGE CENTER

and Cheyennes, some in war costume and other picturesque attire of the days before the white man came; cowboys and freighters with roundup wagons and the emigrant trains; pack outfits and the old stagecoach; all part of an almost vanished era, which the art of William S. Hart, honored guest of the city, has done so much to make re-live through the movie screen," the story continued.[3]

Hart was in town for the dedication of a bronze work representing the Shakespearean actor turned Western movie star and his horse. The *Range Rider of the Yellowstone* was a gift to the city from Hart, and probably his choice of this site for the placement of the piece was based in large part on his friendship with Char-

William S. Hart, Shakespearean actor and star of early Western films, was on hand for the July 4, 1927, dedication of the *Range Rider of the Yellowstone* statue, a bronze depiction of Hart and his favorite horse. Joining Hart for the occasion were Burt Rollins, with the cigar, and sculptor Charles Cristadoro, with cigarette. WESTERN HERITAGE CENTER

The *Range Rider* statue at its present location next to the Yellowstone County Museum. ROB MASSEE

lie Bair and another famous Montanan who preserved the Old West on canvas instead of on screen, Charlie Russell.

At the dedication, Hart gave a short speech in his theatrical way of speaking. It must have been a thrilling moment for the crowd gathered for the occasion when this great star of silent films addressed them.

"My friends," he said, "I can't begin to tell you about how proud I am that any reproduction of me is going to be overlooking this wonderful Yellowstone Valley. If I were asked to describe what the Yellowstone Valley is I would say it is the 'smile of the west.'

"The west! The land of staunch comradeship, of kindly sympathy, of kindred intellect, where hearts beat high and hands grip firm, where poverty is no disgrace and where charity never grows cold; this great, glorious west of ours!"[4]

The *Gazette* reported that Hart spent two hours after the unveiling ceremony shaking hands with the crowd assembled for the event.

The day, which had begun with the arrival of a historical railroad engine, ended with "a gigantic $1,500 display of fireworks at the fairgrounds."[5]

AIRPORT OPENS

Less than a year after the excitement of the forty-fifth anniversary of the founding of Billings, a crowd of five thousand attended the opening of the Billings Municipal Airport atop the Rims on Sunday, May 21, 1928. The celebration was christened "Lindbergh Day," in honor of the young pilot and wing walker who had spent about three months in Billings the previous decade. To carry on the excite-

A seventeen-passenger Douglas aircraft operated by TWA landed at the Billings airport atop the Rims, August 18, 1936. ARTHUR F. SALSBURY PHOTOGRAPH, BOB FEARS COLLECTION, WESTERN HERITAGE CENTER

An early Northwest Airways Sikorsky amphibian aircraft at the Billings airport. This style of plane never made a big splash with the public and obviously wasn't too practical for a passenger line. ARTHUR F. SALSBURY PHOTOGRAPH, BOB FEARS COLLECTION, WESTERN HERITAGE CENTER

CHAPTER THREE BILLINGS IN THE 1920s AND '30s

Train and traffic bridges span the Yellowstone River in 1935. The fairground buildings can be seen in the background. ARTHUR F. SALSBURY PHOTOGRAPH, BOB FEARS COLLECTION, WESTERN HERITAGE CENTER

Mountainview Cemetery drew a crowd for a Memorial Day ceremony in 1930. ARTHUR F. SALSBURY PHOTOGRAPH, BOB FEARS COLLECTION, WESTERN HERITAGE CENTER

Girl Scouts parade in downtown Billings in 1938. Girl Scout troops were organized in Billings in 1926, but they didn't incorporate as the Billings Girl Scout Council until 1939. In 1974, they became Treasure Trail Girl Scout Council. They are now known as the Girl Scouts of Montana and Wyoming. ARTHUR F. SALSBURY PHOTOGRAPH, BOB FEARS COLLECTION, WESTERN HERITAGE CENTER

The Westover Garage also hired an aspiring pilot and wing-walker stuntman as a mechanic when he spent some time in Billings in the 1930s. His name was Dare Devil Slim—better known as Charles Lindbergh. JENSEN COLLECTION, WESTERN HERITAGE CENTER

ment that "Dare Devil Slim" had brought to the city, several stunt pilots were on hand to thrill the crowd, including Grady Woodward of Billings and well-known Montana flier Frank Wiley from Miles City.

When an Airport Commission was established the following year, one of its first acts was to name Dick Logan, who had homesteaded some of the land now part of the expanded airport, as the field's manager. The current Billings airport honors the memory of Logan in its name: Billings Logan International.

Out-of-town visitors who came to Billings for the entertainment available there may well have stayed in the seven-acre tourist park located in North Park, which could accommodate up to five hundred people—and often did in the summer months, when as many as 136 cars per night were parked on the grounds. The park's clientele had the finest services available to them, including "hot and cold showers, gas, electric lights, sewerage, . . . a community hall, two kitchens, four lavatories, a rest room, and four well-equipped cabins," according to the Gazette of November 28, 1928.[6]

(It is interesting to compare what Billings was offering in the 1920s with what the national KOA campgrounds, founded in Billings over half a century later, provide today. It all sounds very similar to the North Park arrangement in the 1920s.)

The city had many parks by 1928, including South and North Parks; Pioneer Park, a thirty-five-acre tract dedicated to the memory of those who founded Billings and the site of Memorial Drive, where fifty-three trees were planted to honor the memory of Billings soldiers (and a nurse) killed in World War I; Highland Park, in the southwest section of town, on three acres donated by the Yegen brothers; and three city ice skating rinks, one on Clark Avenue, one in South Park, and one at Eighteenth and Fourth Avenue North.[7]

Billings had its own radio station, KGHL, which began broadcasting at 7:00 p.m. on June 8, 1928.

DROUGHT AND DEPRESSION

By 1929, Montana had already been experiencing its own depression, brought on by drought and other natural catastrophes, such as swarming grasshoppers that even ate the paint off homes in their paths, but now there was a nationwide Depression to contend with as well, and its effects worsened the situation in Billings and all of Montana. Crops that came to fruition barely paid for themselves as most Americans found their buying power diminished—and in some cases, totally depleted. Stock growers saw their herds' natural feed wither away under blazing suns. As people across the country stopped building because they lacked expendable funds, markets for Montana's lumber resources dried up as well, and when copper prices fell, hundreds of Montana miners and smelter workers found themselves out of work.

CHAPTER THREE BILLINGS IN THE 1920s AND '30s

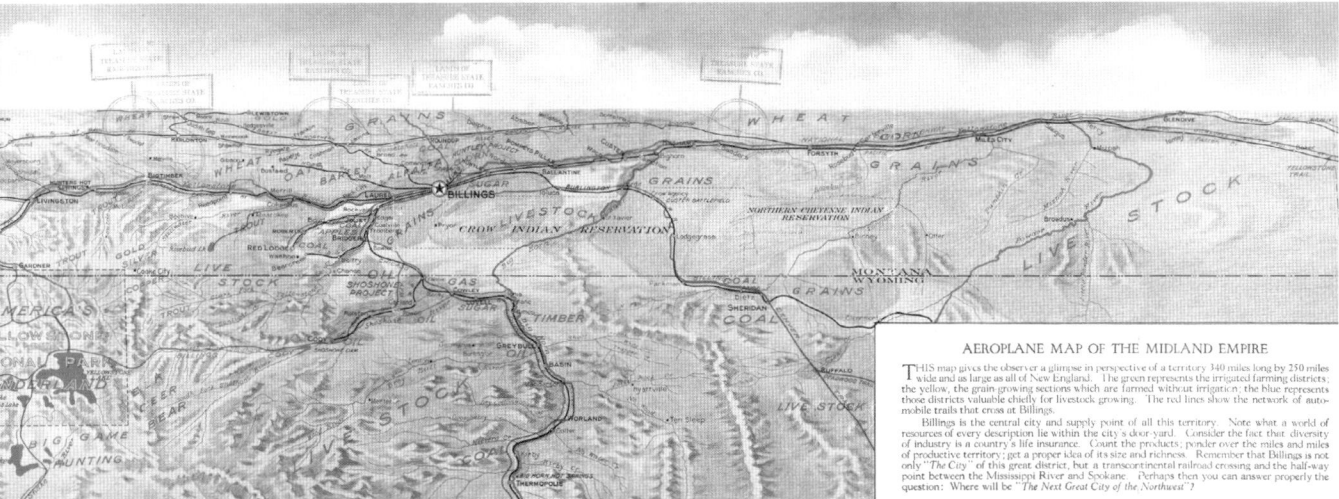

"The Midland Empire" as seen from the air. Billings was predicted to become "The Next Great City of the Northwest."
WESTERN HERITAGE CENTER

Sightseers turned out in 1937 to watch the blasting of the Rims to widen North Twenty-seventh Street or Airport Road. ARTHUR F. SALSBURY PHOTOGRAPH, BOB FEARS COLLECTION, WESTERN HERITAGE CENTER

"Packsaddle Ben" Greenough takes part in a Western Days parade and advertises for Laureleaf Gas, processed in Laurel. Billings had its own "microgas": the Yale Refinery produced the Lightening brand. ARTHUR F. SALSBURY PHOTOGRAPH, BOB FEARS COLLECTION, WESTERN HERITAGE CENTER

Billings was as hard hit as other Montana communities; in fact, beginning in 1927 and continuing through the worst of the Depression years, St. Vincent Hospital was feeding forty to fifty hungry men a day. The Sisters set up a "buffet table" as well as "dining tables," and then left the area to allow the men to enjoy what may well have been their only meal of the day in privacy, realizing that many of the diners felt embarrassed to be accepting charity. Women who came seeking food for their families were given baskets of groceries. Times were hard. It must have seemed at times as though the "magic" had left the city.

ATTEMPTING TO LIFT SPIRITS

The Midland Empire Fair committee felt the need to provide some distraction from the economic and emotional worries of Montanans in 1929. They went all out to make the fourteenth annual fair the most elaborate and entertaining yet. Railroads offered reduced rates for out-of-town fairgoers, and a "season ticket" for the

A number of Billings youngsters are ready for a buggy ride on Lewis Avenue in 1936. The passengers include Betty and Oscar Baltrusch, Patsy Cohe, Bill and Joe Brust, Wayne Berry, Jerry Zimmerman, and Lee, Arthur, Edna, and Frank Salsbury. ARTHUR F. SALSBURY PHOTOGRAPH, BOB FEARS COLLECTION, WESTERN HERITAGE CENTER

Youngsters like Buck Hudson found the lure of a saddled horse hard to resist when they visited the original fairgrounds, now North Park. WESTERN HERITAGE CENTER

Members of the fire department on parade in downtown Billings. ARTHUR F. SALSBURY PHOTOGRAPH, BOB FEARS COLLECTION, WESTERN HERITAGE CENTER

five-day event was only two dollars, with children twelve and under free.

J. M. Bresnahan, manager of the fair, shared his thoughts on the importance of the fair with the *Yellowstone*, a newspaper in Worden, Montana:

> An entertainment program for the five days and nights of the fair will exceed anything ever before attempted at the Midland Empire Fair. It will be more varied and boast of greater novelty than any of the fair entertainment programs which have been uniformly good every year. In addition to the regular daily amusement program, which will fill every hour of the afternoon, there will be four nights of fireworks. A boxing show, to be staged by the American Legion, will be the feature entertainment of the fifth night. . . . There will be four bands, numbering 150 musicians, to furnish music. The amusement program contemplates expenditures of $20,000, in order to make certain that there will not be a single dull moment for the fair visitors. A monster rodeo will bring together rodeo stars from all parts of the west.[8]

Horseback Indians, including Crow Chief Plenty Coups, line the street in front of the Stapleton or original Hart-Albin Building at Broadway and First Avenue North. This part of the building later housed the Hart-Albin Men's Store. ARTHUR F. SALSBURY PHOTOGRAPH, BOB FEARS COLLECTION, WESTERN HERITAGE CENTER

Obviously, no one was going to have a spare moment for those five days to be concerned about the plight of the local or national economy if the Midland Empire Fair committee had its way.

LOOKING BACK

In 1977, William Melville MacDonald, who came to Billings in 1926 and worked at the Sawyer Store until he purchased the Home Bakery in 1938, wrote the following to his granddaughter, Lee Ann MacDonald Bourcier. His words surely reflect the spirit and the mettle of those men and women who rode out the hard times in Billings and elsewhere in the country.

> Looking back ninety years, I am thankful that some greater intelligence blessed me with a gentle, loving, thoughtful companion, fine children, and much love. After all, that is a successful life.[9]

MacDonald was also a poet, and the following poem may well speak to one of the consolations of living in Montana, even when times are hard. A good fishing hole provides not only recreation, but also food for what might otherwise be a rather barren table. (Hunting and fishing were important ways that homesteaders kept food on their tables; in fact, a good many areas around Billings were "hunted out" and had to be painstakingly restocked with game animals and birds by later generations.)

The Westover Garage served not only Billings residents but also tourists on their way by auto to Yellowstone National Park, as the Yellowstone Trail signs visible behind the name of the business attest. JENSEN COLLECTION, WESTERN HERITAGE CENTER

The first Elks Club became the Commercial Club where several single men had rooms and then the Chamber of Commerce Building. In later reincarnations, it housed at least two popular restaurants. Note that North Twenty-seventh Street ends at the Rims; the Airport Road extension had not yet been added. ARTHUR F. SALSBURY PHOTOGRAPH, BOB FEARS COLLECTION, WESTERN HERITAGE CENTER

The perils of early roads illustrated by the "hogsback" drive to Molt, west of the present site of the Yellowstone Country Club. ARTHUR F. SALSBURY PHOTOGRAPH, BOB FEARS COLLECTION, WESTERN HERITAGE CENTER

The Moss yard sports haystacks after a mowing of the grounds around the home. ARTHUR F. SALSBURY PHOTOGRAPH, BOB FEARS COLLECTION, WESTERN HERITAGE CENTER

Give Me

by William M. MacDonald

A trusty friend and a feather fly
A rippling stream, the tang of pine
Some fleecy clouds in an azure sky
A fishing rod, a reel and line
Watch rainbows leap see water cast
Like diamonds from their crimson sides
A reel that sings when hook sets fast
Feel line flow through agate guides
To watch insects skim on a lazy pool
Hear birds twitter as they wing by
To wade the surging waters cool
As hungry trout for flies leap high
The urge returns as sure as fate
I'm young again it's the same old glow
For in that riffle trout lie and wait
The outdoor is calling; I must go.[10]

THE DIRTY THIRTIES IN BILLINGS

Times were tough in Billings as they were everywhere in the country in the 1930s, although Montanans in general may have fared better than most because of the rugged existence many of them were used to as a way of life. Still, few people were lucky enough to escape the far-reaching effects of the Great Depression.

Ernest Hemingway spent seven weeks in St. Vincent Hospital in 1930 with a spiral fracture of his right arm following an automobile accident near Park City. Fellow author John Dos Passos and Floyd Allington, a wrangler at the L–T ranch, where Hemingway had been staying while working on *Death in the Afternoon*, were with Hemingway when his car went into a ditch. COURTESY JOE ALLARD, WESTERN HERITAGE CENTER

Will James was a well-known author and artist who divided his time between a ranch near Pryor and his home in Billings. The city of Billings has honored his memory by naming a school (Will James Junior High) after him and the street on which he lived after his most beloved novel, *Smoky*, although the street name is misspelled as Smokey Lane. SNOOK COLLECTION, WESTERN HERITAGE CENTER

A FAMOUS VISITOR

In the fall of 1930, noted author Ernest Hemingway was injured in an automobile accident west of Billings and brought to St. Vincent Hospital by a passing motorist. Hemingway had been on his way to the Magic City to drop off fellow author John Dos Passos, who was uninjured, to catch a train to New York. With that accomplished, Hemingway and his second passenger, wrangler Floyd Allington, were to continue driving to Florida for some ocean fishing. Allington suffered a dislocated shoulder, but Hemingway's injury, a spiral fracture of the right arm, could have been a career-ending problem if he had not been fortunate enough to receive treatment from Dr. Louis Allard.

Nonetheless, he had to spend seven weeks in the hospital where the only distractions from pain and boredom were provided by a rented radio, Sister Florence Cloonan, a hospital administrator who brought him his mail and talked sports with him, and visits from Earl Snook, a local businessman and friend of artist/author Will James, who provided him with "spirits." Hemingway later wrote a short story based on this experience, "The Gambler, the Nun, and the Radio."

SOME HOPEFUL SIGNS

Billings was still seen as a prospering community in some circles, however. In the January 1931 issue of *Stanolind Record*, a publication of the Standard Oil Company, "Billings: Beets and Beans" explains that "Sugar beets and beans are justly regarded in Billings and the large territory of which it is a center as an asset of greater value than the $5,000,000 they annually bring to this region.

"More than just crops which enter the markets, these two commodities are a symbol of stabilized farming and actually furnish the flow of cash upon which business here depends and thrives.

"With agriculture in its various phases of irrigated and non-irrigated farming and livestock production, well diversified and highly developed, constituting the basic resource and largest income of this territory, beets and beans occupy a unique position. In all of this complex agricultural production they may be compared with preferred gold bonds in the field of investment—not flashy, but conservative and above all, reliable."[11]

Some entertainment at the Babcock Theater. Several Billings clubwomen promoted amateur dramatics in the community in the 1920s and '30s. WESTERN HERITAGE CENTER

The art deco Fox Theater, which would become the Alberta Bair Theater in the 1980s after a $5 million renovation, opened in 1931. Two years later, the Billings Civic Orchestra, a forerunner of the Billings Symphony Orchestra, was formed, and on February 11, 1934, it gave its first performance at the Fox.[12]

Helen Covert, one of the first ushers at the new theater, recalled how exciting it was the night the theater opened its doors for the first time. "The ushers were all decked out in our orange and white uniforms with their bell-bottom pants and shiny brass buttons on the jackets. Mr. Coffman and Mr. Eccles, local florists, had given us each a corsage to wear. Two of us were stationed at each door, and two on each side of the balcony."

Covert said that Billings had its share of top-flight entertainment in the thirties and forties, with two theaters (the Fox and the Babcock) bringing in road shows in addition to films. (A third theater, the Regent, was mainly a movie house.) Fanny Brice played at the Fox, and so did Ethel Barrymore and Barbara Stanwyck.

On January 30, 1933, Amelia Earhart visited the Billings airport for two hours to help launch Northwest Airline service to the Magic City. She drew a large crowd of fans, including young Marjorie (Marj) Logan, whose father, the field's first manager, was often called into service to shoo wildlife off the runway because of the close proximity of the Logan home to the airport.

Marj Logan started flying at age twenty-three; in 1943, at twenty-six, she responded to a radio appeal: "My name is Jacqueline Cochran, and I want you to join the WASPs and learn to fly planes for the Army." The WASPs were Women Airforce Service Pilots during World War II, fliers who ferried planes across the United States and Canada in order to free male pilots for combat missions. Thirty-eight WASPs died while serving their country.

Marj flew B-52s with the Third Ferry Command out of Michigan. After the war, she returned to Billings and joined the Air Force Reserves from which she retired as a major. She and her husband, Kenneth Rolle, were also active in the Civil Air Patrol.

PROHIBITION ENDS

As exciting as it was to have the famous aviatrix at the local airport, probably the most widely hailed event of 1933 in Billings—and around the country—was the lifting of Prohibition. Billings had a very active chapter of the Women's Christian Temperance League, which kept a sharp lookout for infractions of the law, including the sale of "spirits" for "medicinal purposes" by local druggists. (This group of women also performed many a charitable act for residents who were in need; when they were not protesting the sale and consumption of alcohol, they were providing clothing and food for the less fortunate.)

The McCormick Hotel and Billings Brewery, about 1930, across Montana Avenue from the Union train station. WESTERN HERITAGE CENTER

The headline in the morning edition of the *Gazette* on April 7, 1933, proclaimed "Sale of Beer to Start Early Today." That meant that the Billings Brewing Company, which had ceased production of beer and instead had been bottling soft drinks, could restart its operation. Unfortunately, nationally known brands were becoming more and more available, and the Billings enterprise closed in 1951. However, following a new nationwide trend, a number of local or "micro" breweries have recently opened in the city.

A REAL CAMPUS FOR THE NORMAL SCHOOL

In 1935, after a series of delays, ground was finally broken for the first permanent structure on the Normal School campus, a four-story building, counting the tower, which would house the administration offices, classrooms, a library, and an auditorium/gymnasium, as well as other essential elements of a campus, such as a bookstore. On December 3, 1935, when the building was ready for occupancy, some three hundred faculty, students, and well-wishers left the school's downtown quarters and paraded up North Thirtieth Street to the campus, led by the school band.

The following month saw the opening of a new Billings business. According to the *Billings Gazette* of September 17, 1960, "The National Airplane and Motor Co. had its plant at 4th Ave. N. and 27th

Street, and announced orders for a 'tear drop' plane from many states and three foreign countries within four months after it opened in January 1935."[13]

The entrepreneur behind this airplane company was A. B. Green, the designer of the "Bluebird," a small two-passenger plane costing less than $1,000. Green employed eight workers at his plant, but they only completed four planes before the business closed down. Mr. Green then took a job teaching at Billings High School.

A month after the airplane factory opened, the original Babcock Theater was destroyed by fire. Fortunately, the patrons who had gathered there for a boxing match—a crowd estimated at a thousand—escaped without injury, and the Babcock was rebuilt within the year.

THE YALE OIL FIRE

On July 26, 1936, the city suffered a devastating loss of lives and property when the Yale Oil plant, east of Billings, caught fire as the result of a spark from a welding torch that ignited vapors in a crude oil tank. Four young workers died in the conflagration: Jake Walker, 27; Ralph McDermott, 18; Ersie Hiber, 37; and Leon B. Smith, 24. Smith's brother, Lucien, a new Billings firefighter assigned to his first major fire, was on the scene until the fire chief ordered him to return to the firehouse.

According to the *Billings Gazette* of July 27, 1936, "Tears welled into the youthful fire-eater's eyes. 'I guess I lost a brother in that inferno, chief,' he said, trying to keep from crying."

The *Gazette* also noted that "thousands" of the city's estimated twenty-three thousand residents, rushed to the scene to watch the heroic attempts to extinguish the blaze, which was sweeping from oil tank to oil tank until ten were turned into vats of "boiling oil."[14]

The Yale Refinery fire sends thick black smoke over Billings on July 27, 1935. The refinery was located southwest of the MetraPark area. ARTHUR F. SALSBURY PHOTOGRAPH, BOB FEARS COLLECTION, WESTERN HERITAGE CENTER

The aftermath of the Yale fire. The city mourned the loss of four employees of the company, including Leon B. Smith, twenty-four, whose brother was fighting his first fire as a member of the Billings Fire Department. ARTHUR F. SALSBURY PHOTOGRAPH, BOB FEARS COLLECTION, WESTERN HERITAGE CENTER

Philip Fortin, then vice president of Yale Oil, was injured in the fire but recovered from burns on his legs and continued in the oil business, making a fortune. Fortin and his wife, Mary Alice, became significant benefactors to the city, and the Fortin name can be found on many buildings in the area.

The Yale Company was later sold to Carter Oil; the ExxonMobil Refinery is now located on the property.

THE BILLINGS JEWISH COMMUNITY ORGANIZES

In the mid-thirties, three women, Mrs. Dan Kohn, Aurice Solomon, and Mrs. Dave Werner, began holding Friday night religious services in their homes for the Billings Jewish community. (Billings had had Jewish citizens from its founding, but there were no formal services held; in fact, until the 1918 flu epidemic struck the community, members of the Jewish faith who died were taken to Butte for burial. After the epidemic, land was purchased to establish a Jewish cemetery in town.)

The three women eventually persuaded the men who attended the services to raise money for a sanctuary, and in 1940, Temple Beth Aaron was dedicated. Perhaps because it was women who spearheaded the movement for first services and then a sanctuary, it was decided that instead of having women sit apart from men in the Orthodox manner, both sexes would worship together.[15]

THE FLOOD OF 1937

On June 12, 1937, after heavy rains, water from the main canal of the Billings Bench Water Association flooded several areas of the city, including downtown. The Hospital-School, operated by St. Vincent Hospital, was damaged a great deal from the storm, and one of the nuns who was in the building when the flood hit recalled how rapidly the water rose: "We only had about twenty minutes to work on the first floor before the water was so deep we had to leave and keep to the second floor. What damage the water didn't do the awful mud did. It was a night of terror and destruction."[16]

The men seen in the background might have been waiting their turn to have their pictures taken in the kayak a clever photographer provided as a prop for souvenir shots of the flood of 1937. Recently discovered film footage shows a line of people waiting their turn to float and be pictured. WESTERN HERITAGE CENTER

Even though Billings had always had a small population of blacks, including Captain Horace Bivins, the recipient of a Silver Star for his courage in the Spanish-American War, and Walker Browning, the city's first lamplighter, and even had a Twilight Baseball League team called the Colored Giants that played at Athletic Park in the 1930s,[17] racial prejudice overrode common courtesy in 1938 when Marian Anderson was invited to sing in Billings by the Billings Community Concerts Association and was refused a room in the Billings hotels. A local family, the L. R. Aldriches, invited the famed contralto to stay with them.[18] (The following year, Anderson was refused permission to sing in Constitution

CHAPTER THREE BILLINGS IN THE 1920s AND '30s

Downtown Billings on June 12, 1937.
WESTERN HERITAGE CENTER

The fairgrounds were under water during the flood of 1937. ARTHUR F. SALSBURY PHOTOGRAPH, BOB FEARS COLLECTION, WESTERN HERITAGE CENTER

When McMullen Hall first opened in the mid-1930s, students built a bridge across the Billings Bench Water Association Canal to reach campus. ROB MASSEE

A Burlington train crosses the Yellowstone River and leaves Billings, September 1, 1936. ARTHUR F. SALSBURY PHOTOGRAPH, BOB FEARS COLLECTION, WESTERN HERITAGE CENTER

North Twenty-seventh Street in 1920. Note the Mountain States Telephone & Telegraph sign on the telephone building above the Coca-Cola advertisement and the Yellowstone County Courthouse in the second block. WESTERN HERITAGE CENTER

CHAPTER THREE BILLINGS IN THE 1920s AND '30s

The creek in Pioneer Park spilled over its banks during the flood of 1937. ARTHUR F. SALSBURY PHOTOGRAPH, BOB FEARS COLLECTION, WESTERN HERITAGE CENTER

Hall, a building owned by the Daughters of the American Revolution, prompting First Lady Eleanor Roosevelt to arrange for a concert at the Lincoln Memorial. That concert, held on Easter Sunday, 1939, drew an integrated crowd of more than seventy-five thousand, and was heard by millions more on the radio.)

There was good news in 1938 for those who enjoyed outdoor sports events, though. The May 19, 1938, *Gazette* featured pictures of the new Civic Center Park, which boasted a two-thousand-seat stadium and a swimming pool. The $100,000 complex, dubbed Athletic Park, was funded by a partnership between the city and the Work Projects Administration.

As the thirties came to a close, Europe was already feeling the grip of Adolf Hitler, which had been growing throughout the decade, as evidenced in 1933 by Germany's abrupt withdrawal from the League of Nations. Billings, Montana, seemed a long way from the battlefields of Europe, but it would not be long before the country would be embroiled in its second world war in less than a quarter of a century.

Chapter FOUR
BILLINGS IN THE 1940s AND '50s

In addition to the growing concerns about the war in Europe, Billings was dealt an emotional and economic blow on September 11, 1940, when the jewel of the downtown district, the Northern Hotel, was leveled by a disastrous fire.

The loss of the Northern Hotel in September 1940 was a blow to downtown Billings and to Billings' pride. Despite P. B. Moss's pledge to rebuild the landmark hotel, the replacement had little of the grace and grandeur of the original. ARTHUR F. SALSBURY PHOTOGRAPH, BOB FEARS COLLECTION, WESTERN HERITAGE CENTER

The day following the fire, residents gathered to view the still-smoking remains, even double-parking (left-hand side of street) to look at the rubble of a once grand hotel. ARTHUR F. SALSBURY PHOTOGRAPH, BOB FEARS COLLECTION, WESTERN HERITAGE CENTER

The fire apparently started in the late afternoon in the basement area of the Jane Drake Dress Shop, one of eleven businesses operating in the hotel. Within an hour and a half, the mezzanine was fully engulfed by fire, and by shortly after 7:00 p.m., flames came shooting through the roof of the four-story building. Fortunately, no one was seriously injured, as all the hotel guests were safely evacuated, but many a spectator watched the blaze through tears, recalling the glory days of the hotel when European royalty and high-ranking officials of the United States government, as well as well-known entertainers, had stayed there. It was said that the glow from the fire could be seen for fifty miles, but the Northern's reputation as one of the finest hotels in the region was known far beyond that distance.[1]

In a front page editorial on September 13, the *Gazette* reminded its readers of a sad comparison; the headline read "Hotel Fire Brings City Taste of Civilian War," and the text went on to say that the fire "gave the residents of this city a taste of the kind of warfare that has engulfed Europe for more than a year and has brought the destruction of many European cities."[2]

John Rogers, a former history teacher, recalls watching the Northern Hotel fire from a room at St. Vincent Hospital where he was recuperating from surgery following a fracture of the right femur. He was four years old at the time.

"One evening," he recalled, "a nurse came into my room, cranked up my bed, and wheeled me south across the hallway to an empty room so I could look at the pretty fire.

CHAPTER FOUR BILLINGS IN THE 1940s AND '50s

The alley behind the Northern Hotel shows the devastation left in the wake of the fire that destroyed the structure.
ARTHUR F. SALSBURY PHOTOGRAPH, BOB FEARS COLLECTION, WESTERN HERITAGE CENTER

71

At six o'clock, September 12, 1940, the remains of the Northern Hotel still smolder in the early morning light.
WESTERN HERITAGE CENTER

The hotel's chimney still stands. ARTHUR F. SALSBURY PHOTOGRAPH, BOB FEARS COLLECTION, WESTERN HERITAGE CENTER

I watched the Northern Hotel burn for some time before I fell asleep. Of course, I had no idea what this momentous occasion really was. . . . [But] I remember it was quite a blaze."

Three years later, on May 12, 1943, Rogers watched as another landmark Billings building was destroyed by fire. The original St. Vincent Hospital building, which later served as the Orthopedic Hospital School, had been abandoned after it was damaged in the 1937 flood, and the fire that destroyed it was probably caused by children playing with matches, according to fire officials.[3]

Rogers and his mother were among the "hundreds of spectators" who gathered to watch the fire, drawn, no doubt, by "the flames and smoke visible in all parts of the city."[4]

LOSS OF A FAMOUS CITIZEN

When Will James died in November of 1940, the *Gazette* honored the artist/writer with a full-page story in the second section of the November 8 edition, which covered James's life and career in detail. The headline announced "Ashes of Famous Cowboy Author-Artist, Will James, Will Be Scattered Today."

WEATHER WOES

A "smashing snowstorm" hit Billings and most of the state on Thursday, April 17, 1941, according to the *Billings Gazette*, which reported that observers were calling it the worst storm since 1908. "The snow"—which measured 16.5 inches at midnight at the Billings airport—"blocked highways, endangered livestock, damaged trees and shrubs, stopped plane service through Billings, interrupted electric and telephone service, and crushed the O. M. Wold storage garage at 2614 First Avenue South, but brought much-needed moisture to benefit crops and range lands."[5]

The perils of late winter/early spring driving on Clark Avenue, April 17, 1941. ARTHUR F. SALSBURY PHOTOGRAPH, BOB FEARS COLLECTION, WESTERN HERITAGE CENTER

The Billings Brewing Company with a delivery truck loaded with barrels of beer and the company's advertising gem, a "beer bottle on wheels." ARTHUR F. SALSBURY PHOTOGRAPH, BOB FEARS COLLECTION, WESTERN HERITAGE CENTER

Gambling equipment was seized from several Billings clubs in 1947 and destroyed, presumably to protect citizens from the evils of gambling. Sheriff Albert Thomas stands in the middle. WESTERN HERITAGE CENTER

Another noteworthy story shared front-page headlines that day: a report on bombing raids on London. An editorial writer pulled the two stories together the next day.

"Our knee-deep mid-April snow brought mingled expressions of awe and cheer, generated by misgivings as to the fate of livestock on the range, and left not a few with stiff muscles, for there was plenty of work digging out after an all-out attack that seemed 'thousand-fold' by comparison with the skiff-like raids of last winter.

"In this setting we arose Thursday morning to read of London's plight. The British capital had been experiencing its heaviest bombing of the war while from clouds over Billings and the surrounding territory nature was carrying on a silent bombardment that tied up traffic, broke tree limbs, and interfered some with public services.

"The circumstances were but remotely analogous, yet one's thoughts could easily have turned to the troubles of the stricken Isles as he went about the task of clearing the yard of broken limbs and the sidewalks of snow. Indeed, while we were performing our not so unpleasant chores, London's millions were picking up broken masonry and surveying charred ruins and tragedy."[6]

The editorial writer could have no way of knowing, of course, that just eight months later, the United States would enter the war after the Japanese attack on Pearl Harbor on December 7, 1941. And, as had been the case in World War I, Montanans joined the war effort in large numbers, both in the Armed Forces and on the home front. (In World War I, more Montanans [in proportion to the state's population] served in the military than citizens of other states.)

In World War II, Montana's loss of lives of service men and women was exceeded only by the losses suffered by New Mexico.

Anna Lee Dunning, a student at the Normal School, summed up the effect of the U.S. entry into the war by noting, "The war changed everything." While she was referring to the situation on the campus where "the day after Pearl Harbor, the boys were all cleaning out their lockers, and the girls were all crying," her words reflected the situation in Billings and across the country. In ways large and small, *the war changed everything.*

Certainly, the war changed the lives of home front women across the country and in Billings. Anna Lee Dunning's sister, Mina Rose, graduated from the Normal School in 1943

Although the Billings Brewery building disappeared from downtown in 1959, a number of other breweries have opened in recent years, including Montana Brewing Company Brewpub, located in the former Montana Power Building in downtown Billings. ROB MASSEE

and joined the Navy, where she learned to fly; like many other women pilots, most notably the WASPs, she ferried equipment and personnel to free male pilots for combat duty. Other Billings women, housewives and store clerks before the war, joined the ranks of Rosie the Riveter at war production plants both in their home community and elsewhere, or became active members of such organizations as the Red Cross. In fact, with few exceptions, the people of Billings supported the troops in any way they could.

When a call went out for help in harvesting crops in 1942, Dr. McMullen, president of the Normal School, and the few male faculty members and students left on the campus, along with men and women in the community who had never farmed before in their lives, brought in the crops—potatoes, corn, sugar beets. When arrangements were made to bring in Mexican sugar beet workers to join the community of Hispanics who had started working for the Billings sugar processing factory in the 1920s, to assist with future crops, Dr. McMullen started a "conversational Spanish" class at the Normal, so that Billings residents could communicate with their new neighbors. More than two hundred Billings residents took that class. Mexican workers were assisted by Italian and German prisoners of war who worked the beet fields during the last year of the war. A large number of Japanese Americans also were taking on farm jobs left vacant by farmhands who were serving in the Armed Forces—and even teenagers, male and female, were "enlisting" by the thousands as Victory Farm Volunteers.[7]

In July of 1942, Northwest Airlines opened a training center for the Air Transport Command at Logan Field and operated that program for the next year and a half.

That same year, sugar rationing had begun, to be followed a year later by more general rationing of canned goods, meat, butter, dried fruits, and vegetables, etc. Ration books were distributed based on the number of family members and the amount of foodstuffs they already had on hand.[8] Victory gardens sprang up all over town, including plots that were made available to people without their own yards on both the local college campuses. And when Liberty trains pulled into town, there were long lines of Billings citizens eager to purchase war bonds. Whatever they could do, through labor or financial support, they were happy to offer in support of the troops.

In 1942, Kathryn Wright arrived in Billings from Colorado and was immediately hired by the *Billings Gazette* as a general reporter and photographer, as many of the male staff had been drafted. Wright wasted no time in making her mark in Billings, and eventually she wrote for and edited both the entertainment and "society" sections of the paper. When the war ended, she was one of the *Gazette* employees who took the Extra editions to the railroad station and handed them out to soldiers on the troop trains passing through town.

Also in the 1940s, Della Mae Logan became a well-known Billings "businesswoman"; she epitomized for many the "fallen woman with a heart of gold." In fact, when she died, *Gazette* columnist Addison Bragg paid tribute to her, mentioning "the youngsters she helped put through school and the birthday and Christmas presents she saw to it that others would get and the glasses she paid for and the dental bills and the coats and shoes and even college money going to others."[9]

MONTANANS SERVING THE COUNTRY

Montana's Indian tribes were as committed to the war effort as the rest of the state. The day after Pearl Harbor, Barney Old Coyote Jr. hitchhiked into Billings from the Crow reservation and enlisted. He flew fifty combat missions and was the recipient of an Air Medal for his performance as a gunner on a plane that sank a submarine.[10] Frank Redcherries was the first from the Northern Cheyenne reservation near Billings to be sent overseas.[11] Louis Charlo, a member of the Salish tribe, was one of the men who raised the first flag on Mount Suribachi. (A second flag was raised some two hours later; that flag raising was photographed by Joe Rosenthal and is the best-known picture taken during World War II.) Charlo was killed in action a week later.[12] Two days after Charlo's death, Marine Private First Class Richard S. Schiltz, who had captained the 1938 Billings High School Broncs football team to the state championship that year, was also killed in action on Iwo Jima.[13]

At least ten thousand Montanans served in the Navy during World War II, a large number of enlistees from a landlocked state. Commander Wreford Chapple, an Annapolis graduate better known as "Moon" to his Billings family and friends, was promoted to admiral before the end of the war. He was the recipient of two Navy Crosses and two Silver Stars, awarded for "conspicuous gallantry."[14]

Not everyone who served the country went to war, of course. The home front support was vitally important to the war effort, and Billings did its share. The Pacific Car and Foundry Company leased the fairgrounds to house an assembly line operation that produced M-26 tank recovery vehicles. The trailers on which tanks sat for transport were also being produced in Billings, at what had been the Williams Motor Company site. The Pointer-Willamette Company ran that operation. At the same time, the A. N. Metals Products Company was completing fifteen pontoons for the Navy **every day**.[15] (Emphasis added.)

The area coal mines and oil fields were also working at maximum production levels during the war years. And on February 27, 1943, news reached Billings of the Smith Mine disaster in the small community of Bearcreek. Two explosions and the subsequent trapping of a number of miners claimed the lives of seventy-five men that day—hard news for the town itself and the surrounding communities already trying to cope with war news, shortages, and the sorrows that every war brings.

In the July 4, 1943, *Gazette*, a full-page ad urged citizens of Yellowstone County to buy war stamps to build *Shangri-La*, an aircraft carrier, and J.C. Penney's suggested that "What you save at Penney's, Spend with Uncle Sam. Buy War Bonds and Stamps!" Even smaller local ads carried a patriotic message, such as Koppe Jewelers': "Today's Two Best Buys: War Bonds and Koppe Diamonds."

From the number of wedding and engagement stories carried on the "women's pages," readers must have been lining up to buy both. In that same issue, a story recounts that "at a very pretty party, telegrams on a table announced the engagement of Miss Stella Forquer to Chief Specialist Don Foote of Helena. A ship and anchors also decorated the table to carry out the patriotic scheme of the event. (Foote was in charge of Navy advertising for the state.) Another young couple, Arnold V. Larson, twenty-two, and Dorothy Louise Weston, both of Billings, were reported to have taken out a marriage license—even though the price had just been raised to $2.25.

During the war, the *Gazette* ran a column called "With the Armed Services," and on this July 4, it quoted a letter to Postmaster Mearl Fagg from a former Billings mail carrier, John P. Orlando, who was stationed in North Africa: "Believe it or not, about five weeks ago, we got to buy some Pepsi-Cola, and yesterday the American Red Cross brought out some chocolate ice cream. It was swell—the first I've had this year."[16]

Montanans were serving the war effort on every front. According to Gary Glynn, author of *Montana's Home Front During World War II*, "Thousands of Montanans participated in the D-Day invasion and the massive preparations for the landing" on the beaches of Normandy on June 6, 1944.[17]

VE Day—Victory in Europe Day—May 8, 1945, was celebrated somewhat quietly, coming as it did less than a month after the death of President Franklin Roosevelt on April 12. The President's death, followed only six days later by the death of Ernie Pyle, probably the most trusted newsman on the front lines, had shocked and saddened many Americans, and while Montanans were cheered by the news that the European front was no longer experiencing combat conditions, the war in the Pacific raged on.

It took another three months before the emperor of Japan made the decision to surrender to the Allied Forces on August 15, V-J Day. When the news was received, Montana Governor Sam Ford declared a two-day holiday—and tried, unsuccessfully, to have bars and stores shut down during that period of time.[18]

The tragedies of the war were not over for the Billings community, however. On December 8, 1945, a military transport bringing soldiers home from overseas duty missed the approach to the airport and crashed below the Rimrocks. Nineteen passengers and crew members died; four survived. Sister Ann Dolores Muckenthaler, SCL, who was on duty at St. Vincent Hospital that night, recalled how hard the doctors worked to save the lives of the injured, and "what a gloom settled over the city" after the tragedy.

And polio again erupted in epidemic proportions as the 1940s drew to a close, putting a strain on the resources of both Billings hospitals. Rooms and necessary supplies were in short supply, and new patients were arriving daily.

"NORMAL LIFE" GOES ON

Despite war and epidemics, Billings life in the 1940s moved on in a somewhat normal fashion, with local catastrophes and forward-looking projects occurring side by side with war news and home front war efforts. A portion of the South Bridge, constructed in 1898, was washed out in 1944 and rebuilt—for the second time. The same thing happened in 1918—perhaps this bridge had a war phobia—and it had been reconstructed then as well. By 1953 (during the Korean Conflict), however, the city gave up on the old bridge and condemned it.

The old South Bridge during a high water surge in June of 1924. ARTHUR F. SALSBURY PHOTOGRAPH, BOB FEARS COLLECTION, WESTERN HERITAGE CENTER

On the southwestern outskirts of town, Oscar Cooke was assembling his collection of old buildings—which he had moved to his "Oscar's Dreamland" property—antique automobiles, early day tractors, and other interesting reminders of life in years gone by. For more than five decades, this sprawling museum/amusement park was a destination place for people around the state and the country.

PROFESSIONAL BASEBALL COMES TO BILLINGS

With the end of World War II, the Billings community as a whole had leisure time to spend in enjoyable pursuits, and to that end, Robert "Bob" Cobb, who had grown up in Billings before leaving at age eighteen to move to California where he later became well-known as the owner of the Brown Derby restaurant, decided he wanted his hometown to have a professional farm league club. Cobb contacted old friends on the Midland Roundtable, and with the approval of Roundtable president Herb Klindt, Archie Cochrane and Cobb began negotiating the deal.

To meet the needs of a professional team, the city would need a new grandstand. Cobb pitched in $20,000 to kick off a subscription drive to construct a stadium with a regulation baseball field, fencing, and lights for night games. The new team, the Billings Mustangs, would play their Pioneer League games in an impressive setting.

Archie Cochrane was named president of the Mustangs organization; the original board included Billings businessmen such as Russ Hart, of Hart-Albin's, Rockwell Brown, and baseball great Gordon "Mickey" Cochrane, as well as Cobb. Cobb also interested a number of his Hollywood friends in the venture, and stockholders included Bing Crosby, named "Honorary Chairman" of the board, Cecil B. DeMille, Robert Taylor, and Barbara Stanwyck—the star of *Cattle Queen of Montana*, a film that also featured Ronald Reagan. More than 150 people in the Billings community also purchased stock in the venture.

The Mustangs have served as a farm team for several major league teams, including the Cincinnati Reds since 1974. Cobb Field was also home to American Legion teams, the Billings Scarlets and Billings Royals. Through the years, a number of players have "graduated" from the three teams playing at the field to the big leagues, including George Brett and Billings natives Jeff Ballard and Dave McNally. McNally was chosen "Montana's Athlete of the [twentieth] Century" by *Sports Illustrated* magazine, and both McNally and Ballard were named to the "50 All-time Favorite [Baltimore] Orioles" list compiled in 2004 by votes cast by Oriole fans.

After serving the Billings community well for sixty years, Cobb field was razed at the end of the 2007 season and construction began on a new stadium at the same site.

GROWTH CONTINUES AS THE FORTIES COME TO A CLOSE

Although the defense work that had been carried out here during the war was no longer needed, Billings continued to grow as an oil and energy supplier to the region and beyond. In 1949, Conoco opened a new refinery in the community, and the former Yale Oil Company, which had been sold to Carter Oil, became an Exxon refinery (now ExxonMobil). These refineries, along with the Cenex (CHS) refinery in nearby Laurel, continue to employ a number of Billings residents and support community enrichment projects.

Billings was also recognized as an important medical, entertainment, and shopping center for the region—areas of commerce and care that have continued to expand to the present day. And it began to adopt some "big city" ways, such as installing parking meters in the downtown area in 1946.

One ethnic group that had been well represented in the community since the 1880s began to disappear, however. There had been a Chinese population in the area when Coulson was the up-and-coming community on the banks of the Yellowstone. Many Chinese residents had their own businesses in Billings, including restaurants and stores, but by the end of the 1940s, most had moved to the West Coast.[19]

THE 1950S IN BILLINGS

After the hard times of the twenties and thirties and the stressful war years of the forties, the 1950s opened on an optimistic note. New oil and gas fields were being discovered and developed, and for most of the decade, the city enjoyed an "oil boom." Forty-eight oil companies maintained offices in Billings during the 1950s.[20]

But despite the economic boost oil was bringing to the community, all was not serene in Billings; the Korean War took almost twenty thousand Montanans away from home and into battle just five years after the end of World War II. (The Korean War was fought from 1950 to 1953; 350 soldiers from Montana were killed in battle during that conflict.)

Two Billings women, Joan Galles and Wilma Smith, began a drive to restart a League of Women Voters chapter in Billings in 1951. That organization is still active in the community.

In 1951, the 20th Century Fox film *Warpath* was filmed in the Billings area on property owned by the Kuhlman family. *Warpath*, which starred Edmund O'Brien, Dean Jagger, and Forrest Tucker, was just the first of many films to be made in the community or surrounding areas. Others include *Little Big Man* (1970), *The Legend of Walks Far Woman* (1979), *Far and Away* (1991), and *Return to Lonesome Dove* (1993).

Live theater was also available to the Billings community in 1951 through the Pioneer Playhouse, founded by director Frederick Miller and his wife, Marie. For its first two years, the Pioneer Playhouse gave its presentations in Pioneer Park, but the growing popularity of the theater troupe—made up mainly of high school students—started the Millers on a quest for a permanent location. After two years at Wonderland, they were able to move to an actual playhouse on Central Avenue in 1955.

And, to connect Billings to the larger world, television was introduced to the community at 6:00 p.m. on November 9, 1953, by KOOK-TV. By nine, the evening broadcasting period was over and the station signed off—but TV was here to stay. Billings businessman Joe Sample bought the station from the original owners and operated it for a quarter-century. Vic Miller, who had been a voice on KOOK radio, suddenly became one of the most recognizable men in town when he transferred to the television station as one of KOOK's first announcers. Eventually, the city's first TV station began producing its own local shows, according to Billings native Jim Benish, a child at the time, who recalls watching *Yours Sincerely Billie*, a cooking and crafts show starring Billie Lesuer; *Sacrifice Cliff*, featuring Lloyd Larsen, a country singer; and the local news given by Ed Peiss with sports commentary by Red Welch.

And there was plenty of news—and weather—to report. On Saturday, April 2, 1955, Billings received an inch of snow from a wintry storm that was hitting statewide. The weatherman optimistically predicted another inch for the next day. By 2:00 p.m. on Sunday, April 3, the Billings airport had to close, trains and buses were delayed or stranded on impassable roadways, and snowplows could not function because of lack of visibility. The Blizzard of '55 had arrived. Snow continued to fall, and high winds whipped up drifts that reached anywhere from five to twelve feet. Roofs collapsed; cars were abandoned all over town. Neighbors were sharing food and drink with those who had run out of provisions. The city came to a virtual standstill. Old-timers in town still say that the Blizzard of '55 has never been matched in all the years since.

And Nature wasn't through with Billings for the year. July 6, 1955, the "fireworks" of the Fourth continued when a violent hailstorm swept through town, damaging about one hundred planes at the airport, breaking four hundred windows at St. Vincent Hospital, stripping trees of leaves, damaging roofs, and terrifying people who were caught out in cars when the hail came pounding down.

In October that same year, the airport was the site of a different kind of excitement when some fifty thousand people visited there for an Air Fair, which saw a number of

An Electro-Motive stops in Billings and gets the once-over from curious spectators. The McCormick Hotel can be seen across the street at the front of the train. ARTHUR F. SALSBURY PHOTOGRAPH, BOB FEARS COLLECTION, WESTERN HERITAGE CENTER

planes arrive to be part of the display. According to the October 5 *Gazette*, the most popular with the crowd was a B-36 bomber flown in from Ellsworth Air Force Base in South Dakota.[21] The Air Fair also celebrated the dedication of a new 8,600-foot runway by U.S. Representative Orvin Fjare, Governor J. Hugo Aronson, and William Lowe, chairman of the Billings Airport Commission.

Residents of Billings did not need to have special events in town to enjoy their community, however. In the 1950s, Stella and Don Foote established Wonderland, an amusement park that featured a first-rate Western Historical Museum in addition to carnival rides, a trout pond, and boating on the river. The Footes were longtime collectors of Western art and historical artifacts—in fact, Stella toured the world with their "Treasures of the West" collection, which later became the major exhibit material when the Western Heritage Center opened. They also contributed greatly to the area—and the country—when they purchased and preserved the site of Pompeys Pillar, where Captain William Clark of the Lewis and Clark Expedition carved his name on July 25, 1806. Pompeys Pillar was later bought by the government and designated as a National Monument.

Other historical artifacts could be found at the Yellowstone County Museum, founded in 1953, and housed in part in a log cabin that pioneer Paul McCormick built as a guesthouse on his property. Second-generation Billings resident Peter Yegen Jr. saw the possibilities of the cabin and "had it moved piece-by-piece to the airport," his widow, Zellah, told Kimbert Larsen in 1989.[22] In 1988, the museum was renamed The Peter Yegen Jr. Yellowstone County Museum to honor its main benefactor.

A POPULAR BILLINGS LANDMARK BURNS

On August 3, 1956, the main building at the Yellowstone Country Club several miles west of town burned down, destroying the golfing gear of some two hundred members. The *Gazette* of the next day estimated the loss for members' equipment at more than $30,000, and damage to the building at $100,000.

The following month, Billings's Cobb Field hosted the Little World Series, with participating teams coming from Ohio, Washington, D.C., Oregon, and South Carolina. Montana Governor J. Hugo Aronson tossed the first pitch for the opening game.

In 1956, Antoinette (Toni) Rosell, a Billings school counselor, was elected to the Montana House of Representatives and served three terms before she moved to the state senate in 1960. She was the only female legislator in the state in 1969, and in 1975, she became the state senate's first female majority whip.

By the end of January of 1957, the county's supply of passenger car license plates was already exhausted, and more were ordered from the state. In May, Deaconess Hospital announced plans for a one-million-dollar expansion, and St. Vincent Hospital was adding thirty thousand square feet of hospital patient and service area to that facility. By August, the public schools had eleven thousand students enrolled.

As 1957 came to a close, the Gazette was reporting "continuing growth" in Billings and the surrounding areas. A headline in the December 29 edition announced "Billings Area Continues Growth in Population, Industry During Past Year." The story put the population of the city proper at sixty-five thousand, with another five thousand in "adjoining residential areas."[23] Those "adjoining" areas prompted the city-county planner, Ronald Thompson, to comment that Billings had been hard hit by "urban sprawl," an observation that was borne out by an announcement from Paul Covert, president of the Bench Association for Water that "test wells along the Yellowstone River east of Billings indicate a feasible source of water for the Billings Heights."[24]

With such a large population, it was probably no surprise that the same story cited an increase of 46.8 percent in retail business over the last decade—"accounting for 10.9 percent of Montana's total market."[25]

The oil business continued to be a stalwart of the city's success. "Oil production rose in the Midland Empire" during 1957. "Sixteen fields showed increases, the rate of increase being 8,865 barrels a month. Refinery of crude at the three plants in the Billings area—Carter, Continental, and Farmers Union Central Exchange (Cenex)—likewise rose. During the first nine months of the year, the rate of refining was 1,487,885 barrels monthly."[26]

To keep up with the growing population in the Magic City, Lewis & Clark Middle School opened in 1956, followed by Will James Middle School in 1957. Two years later, Billings West High School was built, bringing the number of high schools to three: Senior, West, and Central. (A fourth high school, Skyview, would not open until 1987; it serves the Billings Heights area.)

Despite its continuing physical growth and, some might say, sophistication, Billings still celebrated its frontier past. On June 22, 1957, a crowd of forty thousand turned out to applaud the Western Days Parade.[27]

The 1940 Western Days Parade makes it way through downtown Billings. ARTHUR F. SALSBURY PHOTOGRAPH, BOB FEARS COLLECTION, WESTERN HERITAGE CENTER

On July 2, 1958, Billings experienced its first confirmed tornadoes since the city's founding: two twisters struck at 5:05 p.m. and 5:45 p.m., ripping off roofs and inflicting heavy damage in the city and the surrounding area. Cherry-sized hail accompanied the storm, and by the next day, losses were reported to be approximately $5 million for damage to buildings, cars, and crops. That storm sent several people to the hospitals with cuts and bruises; it flooded a number of basements and ruined lawns when 1.8 inches of rain fell in the course of the storm and caused irrigation ditches to overflow. Windows were broken all over town, and large billboards were blown down. The tornadoes occurred less than a month after a heavy rain/hail event on June 7; between the two storms, officials felt the total storm losses for the years would be "considerably over the $9 million mark."[28]

In 1959, Billings experienced three big shake-ups, one a civic expansion that was challenged, the second a musical hit, and the third the result of a natural disaster.

Sally O'Malley Coffman and Larry Bennett won commemorative spurs as the first queen and king of the Billings Western Pageant and Parade in 1946. "Western Days" provided a yearly reminder of Billings' frontier past—until 2007 when the traditional event inexplicably disappeared from the calendar of events. WESTERN HERITAGE CENTER

In May, the city council voted to annex areas to the west of the current city limits, thus increasing the population of Billings by ten thousand people. As soon as the vote was taken, city fire and police protection was extended into the "new" parts of the community. However, some residents protested the annexation, and it was September before it was declared valid.

Chan Romero, the son of migrant beet workers, formed a band in Billings known as the "Bel-Tones." After the tragic loss of rising star Ritchie Valens in a plane crash, Don Redfield, a Billings disc jockey, sent a tape of the Bel-Tones to Bob Keane, Valens's manager. Keane signed Romero to a contract, and in July of 1959, the Billings musician hit the big time with "Hippy Hippy Shake."[29]

On August 17, a "sharp quake" shook Billings at 11:00 p.m. The first tremor lasted thirty to forty-five seconds, and a second was of shorter duration. The quake, which originated in the Yellowstone Park vicinity of what is now known as Quake Lake, was felt across Montana and into Idaho and Washington state as well, and took many lives when a campground was buried under falling rock.[30]

Chapter FIVE
BILLINGS IN THE 1960s AND '70s

DESTINATION: BILLINGS, MONTANA

The 1960s saw growth and the subsequent problems that often accompany an increase in population—and Billings was not immune to the larger and momentous changes taking place all across the country.

MetraPark hosts rodeos, graduation ceremonies, concerts, and prayer meetings, among other events, in the course of every year. ROB MASSEE

A youngster with a toy train in tow is dwarfed by the Northern Pacific's North Coast Limited. WESTERN HERITAGE CENTER

In 1960, the city census was up, and while Mayor Carl Clavadetscher was happy over the success of both agricultural pursuits and the performance of the oil industry in the Billings area, he was not happy with the "traffic problems" that resulted from increased activity in Billings proper. Nonetheless, he suggested "continued annexation" should be considered—and he predicted a population of 300,000 in the future.[1]

The booming oil industry was certainly cause for such optimism. In 1960, the oil business in Montana grew by 4 percent, and gas sales were up as well. The addition of a new pipeline constructed by the Continental Oil Company, which would run through the refining cities of Billings and Laurel, was another reason for a rosy outlook, and a number of oil companies moved their exploration offices to Billings, adding, as Addison Bragg noted in a story headlined "Oil Industry Booms in 1960,"to [Billings'] status as an oil center."[2]

The entire region was also benefiting from a comparatively new industry: recreational skiing at the newly opened Grizzly Peak ski area in Red Lodge, only an hour away. The influx of out-of-staters—and the number of locals who took up the winter sport—caused what the Gazette called a "minor business boom" in Billings, where stores began stocking ski clothes and equipment. A number of buses ran between Billings and the ski area, and hotels, restaurants, and places offering evening entertainments, such as movie houses and theaters, also enjoyed increased revenue.[3]

In October of 1960, Richard Nixon, who was campaigning for the presidency on the Republican ticket, visited Billings. Nixon drew large crowds at two events; when he spoke from a platform erected in front of the First Avenue entrance to the North-

CHAPTER FIVE BILLINGS IN THE 1960s AND '70s

Above: This view from the top of the courthouse shows the west point of the Rimrocks to the left and "Yegen's Bluff" (Four Dances Cliff) to the right. ARTHUR F. SALSBURY PHOTOGRAPH, BOB FEARS COLLECTION, WESTERN HERITAGE CENTER

Left: The Boys Club of Billings, established in 1971, is now the Boys and Girls Club of Billings. BOYS AND GIRLS CLUB COLLECTION, WESTERN HERITAGE CENTER

ern Hotel, some five thousand people filled the street and sidewalks to cheer him on.[4] (Other visiting dignitaries had also spoken from the first Northern Hotel in the past.)

Some of the great optimism of 1960 dimmed a bit in 1961, a year of drought and grasshopper invasions over the spring and summer months followed by some of the heaviest snows the area had seen in years during the winter of 1961–62.

On January 25, 1962, Governor Donald Nutter, two of his top aides, and three crew members were killed when their plane crashed in a heavy storm. Lieutenant Governor Tim Babcock, a former Billings businessman, succeeded Nutter.

Nineteen sixty-two saw Eastern Montana College claim the Montana Collegiate Conference basketball championship and the Billings Legion baseball team, coached by Ed Bayne, take both state and regional titles.

Tourists and locals contributed to a record number of visits to the Yellowstone County Museum in 1962, with 18,303 people visiting the collections on display there. And expectations remained high for economic growth and stability in 1963. Construction of new homes and business properties was expected to continue at a brisk rate; oil and agriculture were also expanding endeavors. In addition, not too far down the road to the south, some eight hundred workers at the Yellowtail Dam site looked to Billings for entertainment and shopping.[5]

A view of the city from the Rims, 2007. ROB MASSEE

The city of Billings welcomed President John F. Kennedy on September 25, 1963. A huge crowd greeted his arrival at Logan Field accompanied by Senator Mike Mansfield and Congressman Lee Metcalf. Another seventeen thousand packed the grandstands at the Fairgrounds to hear him speak, and another large crowd was on hand to see him off on September 26. On the morning of his departure, the *Gazette* ran a short front-page story about Kennedy's upcoming trip to Dallas.

The people of Billings were stunned, saddened, and shaken by the young president's assassination. Dr. William Ensign, a physician at St. Vincent Hospital, summed up the shock of the event when he said, "That's not the way we do things in this country." Unfortunately, in the years following, civil rights leader Dr. Martin Luther King Jr. and the slain president's brother Robert F. Kennedy were also assassinated.

On December 22, 1963, Governor and Mrs. Tim Babcock left Montana to travel to Los Angeles where they would launch the celebration of Montana's Territorial Centennial year. The Montana Centennial Band, made up of musicians from around the state, were not only playing in the Rose Bowl Parade but also giving a concert at Disneyland. The state also had a float in the Rose Bowl Parade on January 1, 1964.

Nineteen-sixty four saw more than four hundred new oil wells drilled in Montana, twenty-three new fields discovered, and Billings as "the center of state oil offices," according to Liz Wilson of the

Gazette. Wilson also called 1964 "the best drilling year since 1955" and saw the prosperity of the city clearly indicated by the fact that "$27 million more cleared Billings' banks in '64 than in '63." In addition, Billings building permits were up 22 percent, and the Great Western Sugar Company had also enjoyed an above-average production year. Some three hundred new manufacturing jobs had been created in the city over the year, and some of the "old stalwarts" also saw increased revenue, including the Billings Union Station, with a 6 percent jump in rail travel, making it "the top revenue station between St. Paul and Seattle."[6]

Unfortunately, to counter all the good news on the home front, America was once again embroiled in foreign conflict, this time in Vietnam, and a number of Montanans were again serving their country a long way away from it. Many Montanans were lost in this war, and Lieutenant Commander Rodney Knutson of Billings, who had been a student at Eastern Montana College, was held as a POW for seven years, returning home in 1973 at the war's end. During his captivity, a tree was planted on the Eastern campus in his honor.

A number of the events taking place around the country in the mid- and late 1960s did not cause much of a ripple in Billings. The stirrings of the civil rights movement were not in the forefront, and even the few Vietnam War protests—marches from the EMC campus to the courthouse lawn in downtown—went generally ignored. The oil and gas industry continued its growth spurt, no doubt contributing to the comfort-level of the community.

Billings ended 1965 locked in frigid temperatures (the daily highs were all below zero!) and several inches of snow on the ground, but the chill in the air was replaced with a glow of pride when the

Black Otter Trail on the Rims, taken from the air in the 1930s. From 1957 through 2006, the trail was the site of the Black Otter Hill Climb, a car race which drew a number of drivers and spectators every year. ARTHUR F. SALSBURY PHOTOGRAPH, BOB FEARS COLLECTION, WESTERN HERITAGE CENTER

Black Otter Trail in 2007. ROB MASSEE

Montana float in the seventy-seventh Tournament of Roses Parade took the Sweepstakes Prize on January 1, 1966. The float, which featured two gardens, one in summer and one in winter, was also "decorated" with Miss Montana, Dianne Sue Feller, and several homecoming queens from the University System campuses, including EMC's Charlene Merrifield. Well-known radio and television personality Arthur Godfrey, one of the announcers for the airing of the event, greeted the Montana float by saying "Here comes the float from Bob Cobb country," a reference to the Hollywood entrepreneur who spearheaded the drive to bring professional baseball to his hometown two decades earlier.

During the sixties, Detachment One, Twenty-ninth Fighter Interceptor Squadron was based at the northwest corner of Logan Field. Several of the servicemen stationed there took classes through Eastern Montana College. In the 1970s, the Twenty-ninth would host the Apollo 17 astronauts who were training nearby.

In 1966, the Parmly Billings Library found itself the target of criticism for booking a showing of *The Art of the Banjo*, a film narrated by Pete Seeger. Community activist Mrs. Francis (Leona) Deisz objected to the film, saying, "Seeger is a Communist." Despite the protest, the film was shown to an audience of more than one hundred.

The year ended on a high note for the oil business; the December 29 *Gazette* touted the discovery of the Bell Creek field south of Broadus, calling it "the biggest oil producing area in the Rocky Mountains."[7]

Billings residents, along with the rest of the country, were horrified and saddened by the assassinations of Reverend Martin Luther King Jr. on April 4, 1968, in Memphis, Tennessee, and Robert F. Kennedy only two months later. Kennedy, who had broken the news of King's death to a crowd in Indianapolis, Indiana, where he was campaigning for the presidential nomination, was himself gunned down in California on June 5 and died the next day. In one decade—the 1960s—Americans had seen the violent deaths of three of the country's top leaders. Even in a state like Montana, where most pickups had a gun rack in the back window, people were shaken by the violence of the period.

On June 13, 1968, the *Gazette* headline told the story of more storm destruction in Billings: "Killer Wind Storm Lashes Magic City." Once again, there were trees down, power outages, and broken windows. There were some bright moments in '68, though. Two young Billings residents took home titles that year: Karen Frank, Miss Eastern Montana College, was chosen as Miss Montana 1968 (and was named Miss Congeniality, as well—a first for the Montana pageant), and Thomasine Ruth Hill was named Miss Indian America XV.[8]

CHAPTER FIVE BILLINGS IN THE 1960s AND '70s

Above: In what was billed as an authentic reenactment of the Custer Battle—now known as the Battle of the Little Big Horn—Crow Indians, who had actually been on the side of the U.S. Army, "fought" troop reenactors until the "battleground" was invaded by spectators who wanted a better view of the action. ARTHUR F. SALSBURY PHOTOGRAPH, BOB FEARS COLLECTION, WESTERN HERITAGE CENTER

Left: Several people visited the tepees the Crow people were living in at the "battleground." ARTHUR F. SALSBURY PHOTOGRAPH, BOB FEARS COLLECTION, WESTERN HERITAGE CENTER

On May 29, the Parmly Billings Library opened in its new—and much more spacious quarters—in what had been the Billings Hardware Company building, located only a few blocks from its original home, which was to now house the Western Heritage Center. (When the city began considering the purchase of the old hardware store, then-Mayor Willard Fraser tried to convince people to tear down Cobb Field and build a new library on that site—in addition to building a new baseball stadium in the west end of town. The expense of those projects caused the city to opt for the downtown building already in place. The bond for the $996,500 purchase price passed in June 1967.)[9]

Another familiar downtown building got a "second chance" when Senia Hart, businesswoman and Billings historian, refurbished two floors in the Stapleton Building as shops and artists' studios and invited Marie Halone to open her popular Level Three Tearoom. Hart saved a good many properties from demolition or disuse by purchasing them herself and either restoring them or interesting other people in taking them over. The Rex restaurant location in downtown was one such purchase, as was the historic home known as "The Castle."

After the crowd's incursion onto the field of battle, promoters announced that this was the last ever reenactment of the famous fight. In fact, however, the Crow have held annual and highly successful reenactments on their reservation since the 1970s. The train in the background served as a barrier to keep riders on the "battlefield." ARTHUR F. SALSBURY PHOTOGRAPH, BOB FEARS COLLECTION, WESTERN HERITAGE CENTER

By mid-August, good news about the old Parmly Billings Library building surfaced. Instead of being razed, it would become the Western Heritage Center, the new home of the Don and Stella Foote collection, including "priceless guns, Indian relics, personal belongings of Buffalo Bill Cody, Calamity Jane, as well as stagecoaches, an early hearse, and Billings' first fire engine."[10]

Of course the Billings community was as thrilled as people everywhere when the moon landing took place in July of 1969, but there were some ominous signs that all was not well in this community or elsewhere in the country. The assassinations of the decade were fresh in people's minds; events such as Woodstock in 1969 had the older generation shaking their heads and wondering what would become of the country; and even in Billings, a quieter community than many, narcotic use was being recognized as a problem. While there were many advances worth celebrating in science, space exploration, and civil rights, they were counterbalanced—and, for some, overshadowed—by the darker moments of the decade.

THE 1970S

In the Billings community, however, there were still reasons to celebrate. Late in 1970, Ed Bayne, longtime Billings baseball coach, started a drive to send his friend Bill Lazetich, who coached football at Billings Senior High School for more than twenty-six years, and his family to see son and brother Pete Lazetich, a defensive guard for Stanford, play in the Rose Bowl against Chico State. Pete had been a standout on his father's teams while in high school. The Lazetiches were able to make the trip, and Stanford won, 27–17. (And Bayne's Billings Royals had won their sixteenth state American Legion baseball title in seventeen years the previous summer.)[11]

Another Billings sports star, Dave McNally, a graduate of Legion ball and pitcher for the Baltimore Orioles, had a 24–9 season, topped off by his grand slam homer in the World Series.

On April 12, 1970, Arthur C. Clarke, co-author of *2001: A Space Odyssey*, packed the Petro auditorium, with some audience members crowding in two to a seat. Clarke suggested that by the

The spire of the Congregational Church, the first church in Billings, as seen from the top of the courthouse. That steeple now is displayed on the grounds of Mayflower Congregational Church. ARTHUR F. SALSBURY PHOTOGRAPH, BOB FEARS COLLECTION, WESTERN HERITAGE CENTER

beginning of the next decade, people would be able to communicate instantly with anyone, anywhere—and that people would be able to plug in to an electronic library containing all the information in the world. (In addition to his writing career, Clarke was a working scientist and the inventor of the communications satellite.)[12]

On July 4, 1971, Billings saw "fireworks" atop the Rimrocks when the Skyline Club, a popular nightspot, burned to the ground. The club was a familiar sight from the city proper, having started life as a private residence and then serving as a nightclub from 1946 to 1956 when Mike Basile bought it and it became the Bella Vista Club. When it changed hands again in the 1960s, it became the Skyline. Because the club was outside the city limits and was not a subscriber to a private fire service, there were no firefighters to combat the blaze.[13]

The First Congregational Church on North Twenty-seventh Street. ROB MASSEE

LOSS OF WILLARD FRASER

The citizens of Billings lost their colorful, albeit often controversial, four-term mayor when Willard Fraser died on September 20, 1972, while visiting Yellowstone National Park. *Gazette* columnist Roger Clawson paid tribute to Fraser in an article headlined "With Willard Goes an Era":

> Mayor Willard Fraser—dreamer, clown, and politician extraordinary—is dead. With him dies an era in Billings that was his own. Billings has always been a quiet, solid town, a city where color and eccentricity are frowned upon. But Willard gave the city both and threw in a dash of vision. He was a mayor who would rub elbows with the fur coats and silk shirts of the upper north side and break bread with skid row bums on the same day. Billings was his city, and its residents were his children. He frequently said so.[14]

Fraser made national news when he asked that a "Key to the City" he had ceremoniously presented to First Lady Lady Bird Johnson be returned.

A new Montana Constitution was adopted in 1972, replacing the original, which had been in effect since 1889. Billings residents elected to the Constitutional Convention included Dr. George Rollins of Eastern Montana College, who taught Montana history and was given a chance to make some as a delegate.

Also in 1972, two Billings women were elected to the Montana House. Ann K. "Pat" Regan served first in the House and then in the state Senate, and Polly Holmes went on to serve four terms in the House.

One of Mayor Willard Fraser's many innovative ideas for Billings was the Yellowstone River Float, an annual event. JENSEN COLLECTION, WESTERN HERITAGE CENTER

One of the biggest Billings stories of the year was the discovery that the Apollo 17 crew—Mission Commander Gene Cernan, Ronald Evans, and Harrison "Jack" Schmitt, the only geologist to visit the moon—had trained for their upcoming lunar mission in the Beartooth Mountains near Billings. Cernan was the last man on the moon, as Apollo 17 was the last moon shot for the space program, and Schmitt entered their spacecraft first for their return to earth.

In 1973, the Billings Coalition for Women's Rights was formed to work for passage of the Equal Rights Amendment. The group dissolved in 1978 but left a legacy, the Billings Rape Task Force, which they had worked to establish.

The Phillis Wheatley Club, represented by its president, Mrs. James Prince, and vice president, Mrs. W. B. Lacey, donated the ten-volume set of *The Negro Heritage* to the Parmly Billings Library in the early 1970s. The Phillis Wheatley Club of the Montana Federation of Negro Women's Clubs was founded here in 1918. Mrs. Mattie Hambright was their first president.

CHAPTER FIVE BILLINGS IN THE 1960s AND '70s

Billings Mayor Willard Fraser (left front), riding his bicycle in the 1960s, died in office in 1972. WESTERN HERITAGE CENTER

After several years of riding high on a booming oil economy, Billings suffered a setback in 1974 because of the Arab oil boycott. The entire country was suffering from gasoline and heating oil shortages, but Billings, with oil and agriculture as its economic mainstays, was particularly hard hit, and the oil business in the community never fully recovered. Although the three area refineries are still an important part of the economy, a number of oil companies that had offices here began to close up shop, and by the mid-1980s, oil field workers were out of work. (There has been a resurgence of oil activity in the state in recent years.)

In October of 1975, Billings' teachers went on strike; the walkout only lasted twelve days, but the lingering effects caused hard feelings, and several teachers left the district at the end of the school year.

In March of 1976, Montana's longtime senator and senate majority leader for sixteen years, Mike Mansfield, announced that he had decided against seeking reelection. Although he never stood for office again, he continued to serve the country in a number of ways, including as ambassador to Japan.

On October 11, 1976, the city held a bicentennial parade, which was led by Governor and Mrs. Tom Judge, and the next day, the Freedom Train pulled into town with its display of historical documents and other patriotic materials.

A Great Northern train chugs its way out of the Echo Canyon tunnel, west of Billings, close to the present site of the Yellowstone Country Club. ARTHUR F. SALSBURY PHOTOGRAPH, BOB FEARS COLLECTION, WESTERN HERITAGE CENTER

After suffering an economic hiccup in the mid-seventies, prosperity seemed to be returning to the area in 1976 when construction of new homes hit an all-time high. According to Kerry Pechter in the *Gazette* of December 24, 1976, "664 permits for single family dwellings, 51 for duplexes, 284 for fourplexes, and 19 for multifamily buildings" were issued during the year, adding up to 1,182 new housing units for the city. Two-bedroom homes were selling for $31,000 at the time.

Billings also voted to adopt a new city charter in 1976. This charter, which authorizes a hired city administrator position and elected officials to serve as mayor and city council members, took effect on May 2, 1977.

Of course, a pendulum swinging one way has to swing back, and good news is often followed by bad—in this case, the announcement in 1977 by Amtrak that it was planning cutbacks in passenger service in and out of Montana. For a railroad town like Billings, this was a particularly hard blow.

Then, because of the energy crunch, Governor Judge ordered a 10 percent cut in electricity use in all state government buildings and recommended that the private sector follow suit.

Even Nature got into the act, delivering what seemed to be the never-ending winter of 1978–79, with snow beginning in November and never leaving the area until April. The bitter cold not only killed thousands of cattle in the region but also, in the city proper, caused water pipes to burst all over town, creating impromptu skating rinks in several neighborhoods for those who could stand to be out in the freezing temperatures. A number of people had their car tires freeze to their (unheated) garage floors and had to find other means of transportation, such as cross-country skis; a number of frostbitten noses, ears, and fingers required treatment.

In January 1979, Diane Barz of Billings was sworn in as Montana's first female district judge. Judge Barz served as the family court judge for Yellowstone County and adjudicated all cases in Big Horn County.

In February of that year, Montana was flooded with scientists, astronomers, and photographers from all over the world who wanted to get the best possible view of the total eclipse of the sun.

And an apparently repentant Mother Nature made up for the previous winter by sending little snow our way in the winter of 1979–80.

chapter SIX

BILLINGS IN THE 1980s AND '90s

DESTINATION: BILLINGS, MONTANA

On May 18, 1980, Mount St. Helens erupted on the West Coast. By May 19, Billings—and most of the state—was covered in ash, making visibility poor, prompting health alerts for people with respiratory problems, and causing Governor Tom Judge to cancel school across the state for the following day.

On July 14, 1981, a sudden squall line hit Billings with rain and strong winds that shattered the north windows of the Parmly Billings Library. A fast-moving line of wild weather, the storm only lasted about ten minutes—ample time to frighten library patrons who had been quietly reading only moments before the wind and rain came tearing in through the broken windows. Once the storm moved on, library staff and visitors rushed to retrieve books and magazines, some of them drenched, from the affected area. Some of the patrons in the library that day may well have been researching for the decade's biggest event—the celebration of Billings' one-hundredth birthday![1]

The Planning Committee for this momentous occasion included a number of prominent Billings residents, including Russ Clark, chair; Barbara Sample, vice chair; banker Jim Scott, community leaders Lucille Mills, Beverlee Sveinson, Mariam Sample, and Elsie Fergus; Billings businesswoman Senia Hart; the *Gazette*'s Kathryn Wright; businessman Jerry Hanson; historian John Willard; MetraPark director Bob Glasgow; and local television celebrity Vic Miller. Donna Gaub served as the executive director.

Early Billings businessman Paul McCormick had his own herd of elk, which roamed an enclosed area west of town. In this picture, McCormick, the gentleman standing closest to the elk, hosted a "hunting party" for a number of friends. The site is believed to be close to the corner of Seventeenth Street West and Poly Drive in the current city of Billings.
WESTERN HERITAGE CENTER

It was quite a celebration, with a number of commemorative items available as souvenirs of the anniversary, including coins, belt buckles, and art works. A time capsule was buried in the lobby of the Transwestern III building, located on the site of Paul McCormick's home. Rocky Mountain College hosted a Centennial Fair on the campus; all sorts of crafts that would have been employed by the first settlers here were demonstrated and could be tried by anyone in the large crowds which attended who wished to do so. The college also teamed with the Shrine Auditorium to offer "Rendezvous of '82" in August. On July 19, a bronze statue of Frederick Billings was unveiled, to the special delight of thirty-five members of the Billings family in town for the event. (That statue now stands on the grounds of the Western Heritage Center.)

In June, Eastern Montana College's Petro Theater hosted Jurrette's School of Baton & Dance's production of "Hitch Your Wagon to a Star," a centennial-themed show; in July, the college held an interdenominational worship service and in September welcomed the Air Force Band and the Singing Sergeants for a musical salute to the birthday city. The Yellowstone Art Center held a Centennial Art Competition, and the Centennial Postal Station at Rimrock Mall used a special centennial stamp designed by John Kolstad to cancel mail sent from Billings during the week of July 19–23.[2]

From June 20 to 25, the *Gazette* published a series of centennial inserts, looking back over the years since Billings was founded. And on June 25, a centennial wagon train, comprised of eight wagons and twenty-seven outriders, arrived in town to camp for the night at the Indian Caves (also known as the Pictograph Caves). They had started their journey at Yellowtail Dam.

Riverfront Park, dedicated in 1982, is one of the many city parks located along the Yellowstone River. ROB MASSEE

On September 18, a groundbreaking was held for Riverfront Park on Lake Josephine. Dale Hawkins, founder of the Yellowstone Corral of the Westerners in Billings in 1972 and well-known art collector, chaired the Riverfront Park Project, with the able assistance of Vern Prill, of the City Parks Department, and Oscar Chaffee, retired state editor for the *Gazette*.[3] In October, while not a centennial event, the community cheered the re-opening of the Hart-Albin Department Store in downtown, which had been closed for repairs after a fire.

The biggest fanfare, however, was reserved for a huge production at MetraPark of *Yellowstone Hurrah!* written by EMC theater arts professor and well-known playwright Norman Bert. Fred K. Miller, founder of the Pioneer Playhouse in the 1950s, chaired the *Yellowstone Hurrah!* production committee, with Donna Gaub Beutler as executive director. A number of people whose names were very familiar to the Billings theater-going public also played important roles in mounting this "cast of thousands" production. Jurrette Sindelar, a great-granddaughter of Billings pioneer John Dover, and Lindy Coon choreographed the show; Donna Bach was costume designer; Blair Anderson, property master; Hal Hansen, production stage manager; Sally Miller and Katherine Bassett, assistant stage managers; Liam O'Brien, production director; Arthur Brandvold, music director; Mark Cuddy, staging director; and Stephen Krempasky, setting and lighting designer. The show ran August 1, 2, and 13—and wasn't overshadowed by a brief visit to the Centennial City by President Ronald Reagan on August 11.[4]

The year of celebration received a beautiful send-off on Christmas Day, when the *Gazette* ran a full-color reproduction of a painting by their talented artist John Potter of the Moss Mansion, decorated for Christmas in 1902.

One of the oldest buildings in Billings was part of George Henry's restaurant in downtown Billings, which closed in 2009. Originally the family home of Robert Crowe, an expert cabinetmaker, it later became a boardinghouse and a tearoom. Crowe also built the current School District Two building, across the street from his one-time residence, and the McKinley School. ROB MASSEE

CENTENNIAL YEAR ENDS ON A DOWN NOTE

In December of 1982, *Gazette* reporter Mark Ragan informed readers that the city was showing "three years of steadily rising deficits that could top $2 million in fiscal year 1984–85 if the city does not cut services or raise more money." A graph accompanying Ragan's story indicated that tax revenues for the 1982–83 fiscal year would be approximately $7.1 million, increasing to $7.3 million in 1983–84 and $7.4 million in the following year. Other city income from sources such as licenses and permits, fines, and charges for various services were projected to rise by 8.7 percent in 1983–84, and perhaps increase another 3 percent in 1984–85.

Helen Hunkins Hallinan grew up in Billings where her father had a jewelry store on North Broadway. LIBRARY OF CONGRESS, PRESS BUREAU, CONGRESSIONAL UNION FOR WOMEN SUFFRAGE, WASHINGTON, D.C.

Not surprisingly, the biggest ticket budgets were those of the police and fire departments: 3.8 million and 3.5 million in 1982–83, with estimated increases to 4.3 and 4.2 in 1983–84 and 4.7 and 4.1 the following years. (Obviously, just providing police and fire protection would cost more than the annual tax take.) Other public works, parks, city administration, and city courts expenses also needed to be paid from these revenues, leaving little, if any, "wiggle room" for unexpected expenses.[5]

In a move that might have been amusing except for the serious nature of any budget deficit, be it in one's own household or in the city's coffers, the city council determined to meet the challenge head on by stopping the purchase of new books for the library in January of 1983.[6]

Ellen Newberg, head librarian at the time, found a way around the no-new-books declaration by celebrating her husband's fortieth birthday in March with a party at the Parmly Billings Library. Guests were told "no gifts" for husband Alan, but asked instead to bring a new book for the library. It was quite a success.[7]

Billings was still attempting to raise money to buy the Moss Mansion and convert it to a house museum in April of 1983, and that effort was helped along when State Representative Jack Sands managed to present the only amendment that was allowed to the state's long-range building program bill, HB 900, calling for $50,000 to help the city reach its goal.[8]

At the same time, owners of residential properties in the vicinity of Twenty-fourth Street West sued the city over the widening of that street, saying that commercial development in the area soon followed, decreasing the value of their homes. They wanted the city to change their zoning status from "residential" to "residential-professional," which they felt would boost both the value of their property and make it more desirable to would-be buyers.

The *Gazette* reported on April 12 that city tax revenues were expected to drop by more than $500,000 "because of a major decrease in the taxable value of property in the city."[9] The following month, some additional funding was requested through a $1.6 million tax boost in order to increase spending for city services. Three days later, the Teamsters Local 190, which represented 380 city employees, asked for a 10.5 percent raise in wages. Obviously, there was not enough money to answer every need, and by August, the Yellowstone County Commissioners, also feeling the money crunch, were trying to make cuts in the county's $20 million budget.

Hazel Hunkins Hallinan, who grew up in Billings and became a well-known suffragette and journalist, chose to return home to Billings for burial in Mountview Cemetery. ROB MASSEE

Mayor Fraser and his wife, Marjorie, a daughter of poet Robert Frost, are buried in Mountview Cemetery. ROB MASSEE

The economic outlook wasn't brightened when the Montana Power Company (MPC) announced a record-setting rate increase for electricity, nor was the overall mood of the state improved when MPC hired non-union workers for a natural gas pipeline job. That discovery brought about violence and vandalism at the job site.

Another job-related fracas was in the making over the state's hiring preference law, giving special consideration to veterans and handicapped individuals applying for state jobs. A special session of the legislature in December modified the law to make those special considerations only applicable as tiebreakers when two applicants of equal ability are eligible for the same position.

Some of the shine of the Magic City seemed to dim a bit in 1984. The city's hockey team, the Montana Magic, left town when the Central Hockey League folded, leaving a large number of creditors and at least a hundred thousand dollars in unpaid bills. Except for the blow to an already hurting economy, people weren't all that sad to see them go; their record stood at twenty wins, fifty-two losses, and four ties.[10]

The city had increased its population, however, by annexing the Billings Heights area in July.

The following year, recreational possibilities for Billings' residents improved when the state purchased Lake Elmo for a state park. (Lake Elmo, a popular spot for summer fun, including swimming and fishing, had been the site of the Elmo Club, owned and operated by Elmo McCracken until a fire in 1946).[11]

In 1984, the Great Western Sugar Company was put up for sale, a cause for some concern for sugar beet growers. The plant was purchased the following year with no interruption in the sugar refining process.

Another type of vegetation made news in 1984. A "Friday Finishers" column noted, "Kathy Taggart, supervisor of the Billings Police Department's Identification Division, lifted a fingerprint from an onion in a recent robbery investigation.

"Police believed this was the first print ever to be taken from a vegetable."[12]

By midway through the decade, concerns about drug use in the community were growing, with the Chemical People Task Force reporting drug and alcohol use "rampant among Billings youth." Many were said to be "poly drug users," ingesting alcohol, pills, and recreational drugs.[13]

Oil and gas lease sales dropped 50 percent in the Williston Basin area of Montana and North Dakota in 1985, another indication that the oil boom of the previous three decades was over for the time being in Billings.[14]

The state legislature met in special session in June to consider a $100 million shortfall in state revenues. Cuts to the University System meant eliminating twenty full-time equivalent positions at Eastern, including faculty, maintenance, library, and support staff. (The college ended up cutting ten faculty and twelve staff positions.)

The Midland Packing Company, beef processors, closed in 1985. They hoped to re-open the following year, but the state Commerce Department turned down their request for a grant to do so.

In November of 1986, Montana voters approved a state lottery after much discussion of the pros and cons of such a move.

In Billings, construction of a new one-hundred-bed convalescent center, Parkside, began in 1986. The project was estimated to cost $3 million. In addition, the city council set aside $102,000 toward purchase of the Moss Mansion if the community could raise the purchase price of $450,000 by the deadline date for the sale. The goal was reached in December of 1987, and Billings and the state had a jointly owned house museum.

During the 1986 Christmas season, members of Our Lady of Guadalupe parish, located in the southside neighborhood where so many families who moved to Billings to work the sugar beet fields had their homes, took part in a posada, a Mexican tradition. In a procession meant to recall Mary and Joseph looking for a place to stay, the group, carrying lighted candles and singing Christmas songs, went to a home and asked for shelter. At first they were turned down, but then they were invited in for prayers and cookies.[15]

A less Christmasy message was received on December 19, 1986, when Eastern Montana College cut seven administrative jobs from the campus roster in an effort to trim $1.1 million from the school's budget. That announcement was followed on Christmas Eve with the word of additional cuts in the faculty and staff ranks. The state was experiencing budget woes because of state revenue shortfalls caused in part by changes in the federal tax laws, and by the hard times Montana farming and ranching communities were trying to weather.[16]

The private sector was also doing some belt-tightening. Billings Catholic Schools consolidated their schools, housing preschool through second grade and an afterschool program at Holy Rosary School, third through fifth at St. Pius, and sixth through eighth at Fratt. This allowed a one-third cut of their school personnel.

There was a glimmer of hope on the oil front, however. Crude oil had risen in price to $18 a barrel, prompting W. W. Ballard, president of the Montana Petroleum Association, to tell Paul Holley of the *Gazette*, "If OPEC stabilizes prices at $18, that would put the domestic price at about $19 or $20 a barrel. I think you'd see 1987 as a pretty active year in exploration at that price."[17]

That was good news for the adults in Billings, but the youngsters had another reason to celebrate: Gerhart Blain returned to what had been a tradition in Billings for many years—towing Santa and his reindeer across the evening sky behind his helicopter on Christmas Eve.

The good omens some saw for 1987 did not all materialize. In fact, 1987 saw oil prices decline, while the state raised gas and diesel taxes by three cents a gallon. With the advent of legalized gambling—not on the Las Vegas level, certainly, but very popular nonetheless—casinos began multiplying overnight it seemed. By early 1987, local restaurants were complaining that the casinos were cutting into their business by serving lower-priced meals. Several restaurants closed, but new casinos moved into those locations. The city was to receive 15 percent of casino profits, and from July to September of 1987 that amounted to $246,070.

In the spring, faced with the grim news that 5,800 residents of Yellowstone County were out of work, a new campaign was launched for the city—"Billings Is Alive and Doing Well."

And there were some bright moments for the community, both private and public. In the private sector, a gentleman named Ivan Enwall and his wife Dorthybelle had for years been contributing $40 of their monthly Social Security check to help needy children in Billings schools. After his wife's death, when he was in failing health, he put aside $6,000 to carry on their charity. Mr. Enwall died in June, but he continued to help the needy children he cared so much about.

The medical community continued to grow in 1987 with the opening of the Parkview Convalescent Center and construction beginning on the Northern Rockies Cancer Center and a $5.5 million psychiatric hospital building on the Deaconess Hospital campus. But new housing starts stalled, and both Cole's Department Store and F. W. Woolworth moved out of downtown.

Cattle prices rose, and 1987 was, in general, a better year for agriculture than 1986 had been. Fresh produce could be had in downtown, too, with the founding of the Yellowstone Valley Farmers Market.

Still, money was tight. School District Two trustees cut twenty-eight and one-half central staff positions at their December meeting, and by the beginning of 1988, they were considering laying off more than sixty teachers to balance their budget. No wonder the *Gazette* commented that "a lack of jobs and per capita income far below the national average is causing people to leave Montana."[18]

The medical corridor—the area between the two hospital campuses—continued to grow in 1988, but the drought that year was the worst in memory—wreaking havoc with agriculture and setting timber and grasslands ablaze. Over a million acres burned in Yellowstone National Park, and less extensive, but still destructive, wildfires were fought all over the state, including close to Billings.

Two city department heads resigned to take jobs elsewhere. Fire Chief Bobby Williams and Head Librarian Ellen Newberg both moved out of state for new positions, prompting City Administrator Alan Tandy to blame "a growing gap between salaries in Montana and neighboring states" for their departures.[19]

There were still good times to be had, despite the area's economic woes. In May, the Billings-Coulson City Trolley was brought out of retirement, and people could enjoy a smooth ride behind a pair of red roans. In June, the Farmers Market drew crowds of a thousand or more to purchase fresh fruits and vegetables, flowers and herbs, and delectable baked goods from nearby Hutterite colonies. And, as in years past, spirits were lifted by the Fourth of July fireworks display, sponsored this year by the *Billings Gazette*, Burlington Northern, Hart-Albin, Deaconess Hospital, and the Billings Sheraton Hotel. Also in July, athletes from around the state gathered in Billings for the Big Sky State Games. Olympian Kari Swenson lit the torch to begin the competition in nineteen events. A two-day air show brought eighty thousand people to the airport that month, too.

In August, a fledgling ZooMontana sponsored a "Name the Tigers" contest, which brought a number of visitors to the zoo grounds to see the two cubs.

The Sugar Beet Festival in October drew thirteen hundred to a costume "Beet Ball," and the Festival of Trees raised more than $25,000 in December to fund the Billings Council to Prevent Child Abuse.

And the good citizens of Billings did not forget the less fortunate, even if they were in somewhat straitened circumstances themselves. A "Bags of Plenty" food drive in December collected more than two hundred thousand pounds of food for the Billings Food Bank, and Dr. and Mrs. Robert Hagstrom, Dr. David Gregory, and nurses Pat Ellison and Kathy Fowler took ten tons of donated medical equipment to Honduras.[20]

Near the end of the year, the Billings Chamber of Commerce broke ground for their new building on the 800 block of South Twenty-seventh Street, fronting the direct route visitors coming into town from the south or east would take after leaving Interstates 94 and 90.

THE news of 1989 was the Great Montana Centennial Cattle Drive, organized mainly by Billings cartoonist and artist Stan Lynde. Lynde and fellow cartoonist Barry McWilliams started talking about a cattle drive as a way to recognize Montana's one-hundredth birthday as a state in 1987, and they enlisted the help of rancher Jim Wempner early on. But as the Latigo organization—named for one of Lynde's popular cartoon characters—got busier and busier, it was mostly Lynde pushing the program forward.

And what a program it was! Three hundred wagons, thousands of horses and riders, a herd of four thousand cattle, including three hundred Texas longhorns, making a six-day, sixty-mile drive from Roundup to Billings, with numerous "social" events—a "family night" when visitors were welcomed to the camp; trail concerts, some planned, some impromptu; a wedding; visits to the Anheuser-Busch tent (saloon and entertainment center).

Some of the participants were the real thing—drovers and wranglers in their everyday lives—and some were just along for the ride, but all loved the experience, even those thousands who participated only at the end, braving traffic tie-ups and a long, very early morning wait to cheer the group as it arrived in Billings on Saturday, September 9.

It was an event for all ages of participants, whether admiring audience or riders on the trail. The oldest participant was 102-year-old Jess Killingsruth of Sidney, and the youngest was five-year-old Sarah Montana Hart of Virginia, who was accompanied by her father, Kim, who had grown up in Billings. Turk Stovall, thirteen, of Billings was the youngest drover for the event; he had been riding since the age of two and working as a drover for five years.[21]

Sister Marie Carmel Dunning, SCL, who described herself as "an old cowhand," went along as part of the medical team. (In "real life," she was a hospital chaplain, accustomed to dealing with trauma—of which the Centennial Drive was remarkably free.)[22] And Verle Rademacher, owner and editor of the White Sulphur Springs newspaper, brought along a handset press to put out a daily "cattle drive edition" of his *Meagher County News*. The papers sold out every day.[23]

A number of big names were on hand to entertain on the trail, such as Hoyt Axton and Sheb Wooley, and the closing events were held at MetraPark, including an afternoon art show and auction, and musical entertainment available at the Budweiser tent. The Grand Finale was an evening concert featuring Lee Greenwood.

THE 1990s

In 1990, Montana lost a congressional seat when the census turned up only 803,655 residents in the state. The state continues to be represented by a lone member of Congress, currently Representative Dennis Rehberg of Billings.

There was both good news and bad on the economic front in Billings. The Midland Packing Company, which had been operating as Meats of Montana, closed again because of cash-flow problems, and the venerable Hart-Albin's, downtown's anchor store, closed after eighty-eight years. There were some positives, however, including an increase in home construction and some major investments in refineries, including a $140 million coker project at Conoco, which was expected

Alberta Bair was born in Billings in a family home located on the property where the Alberta Bair Theater now stands. Here she attends the opening of one of her favorite charities, the opening of the new Boys and Girls Club on Orchard Avenue.
BOYS AND GIRLS CLUB COLLECTION, WESTERN HERITAGE CENTER

to generate 500 construction jobs, and 50 new permanent positions. (The following year, the number of construction workers had grown to 750, and the predictions on permanent positions had risen to 220.)

Two longtime Billings purveyors of fine music through the years celebrated anniversaries in 1990: the Billings Community Concerts Association turned sixty, and the Billings Symphony, forty. And there was good news for those who supported the effort to enlarge the ZooMontana program. The zoo raised $2.5 million for its expansion plans.

Concertgoers were treated to a number of top-flight popular music groups who visited the Magic City in 1990. Aerosmith, Kiss, and Motley Crue rocked the house at Metra, while the more sedate Gordon Lightfoot and Kingston Trio entertained at the Alberta Bair Theater. Sawyer Brown drew thousands to the annual ZooGrass festival.

A less happy note was the increasing problem of gang activity in the city, and the call-up of local reservists and medical personnel for the first Gulf War.

At the end of the year, Billings Senior and Billings West high schools held "challenge" food drives for Christmas; West won with a total of 3.5 tons collected by their students, and the drive brought in 5.5 tons overall.

Just three days before Christmas, artist and organizer of the Centennial Cattle Drive Stan Lynde lost thirty-two years worth of artwork and original strips of his Latigo and Rick O'Shay cartoons when his home burned down. Fortunately, boxes of books published by his Cottonwood Graphics company were stored in a separate garage and saved—and, more importantly, no one was physically injured.

By 1991, Billings had come through a period of economic recession and was recognized by Money magazine as its #6 pick of "best metropolitan areas" in the country. New housing starts were rising, more jobs were available in the refinery field, and the town was "star-struck" in the spring when a number of locals were chosen as extras in a Tom Cruise film, Far and Away, directed by Ron Howard. Shooting took place in the countryside west of town, in the same area where the cattle drive participants had camped two years earlier, and in the Billings Depot.

Mother Nature put on shows of her own that year, with two bad storms in June. On the nineteenth, a downpour dropped 1.35 inches of rain on Billings in a relatively short period of time, causing the Rims to turn into waterfalls in spots and flooding a number of homes. Two days later, more rain and a tornado flooded north Billings a second time.

CHAPTER SIX BILLINGS IN THE 1980s AND '90s

Billings had reasons to celebrate in 1992. For one thing, the Montana economy was growing and personal incomes were increasing by more than 6 percent. Several large retailers were coming to town, including Wal-Mart and Toys "R" Us, and once again new housing starts were on the rise. Perhaps most notable, however, was the city's designation as one of only ten "All American Cities" by the National Civic League.

Concerts continued to be the entertainment of choice for a number of Billings' residents. Garth Brooks sold out Metra's 10,400 seats for his concert, disappointing about 30,000 others who had wanted to attend. ZooMontana's popular fundraiser, ZooGrass, drew thousands to enjoy Three Dog Night and Lou Diamond Phillips.

Sadly, the city was rocked by tragedy just a week before Christmas when a Cessna Citation carrying a crew of two and six employees of the Western Power Administration office in Billings crashed into the School District Two warehouse as it approached the airport, killing all on board. Investigators believed that they had been caught in the wake of a large jet that had made the same approach ahead of them. (In 1993, the Federal Aviation Administration ordered that pilots be issued wake-turbulence warnings when cleared to land behind Boeing 757s.) No one on the ground was injured.

Billings received more national attention in 1993, this time from an unlikely source: *Cosmopolitan* named it a one of the eight best American cities for women to find a man!

The summer of 1993 provided a number of opportunities for fans to enjoy their favorite sports. More than eleven thousand Montanans took part in the Big Sky Games in July, and in August a crowd of five thousand watched Robbie Knievel (son of Evel) soar 168 feet overhead to break his own "no hands" motorcycle jump record at Lamplighter Square in west Billings.

Not quite that many attended a dedication of the Frederick Billings statue when it was moved to its present location on the grounds of the Western Heritage Center that same month, but a number of the Billings family descendants were on hand for the event.

History repeated itself in September. The first person to cross the new East Bridge was the same person who had been the first to cross the earlier bridge in 1935. At that time, Dick Johnson was a seven-year-old riding his horse; in 1993, the crossing was made by car.[24]

Billings was shocked in December when vandals threw rocks through windows displaying menorahs. The response was an almost immediate coming together of the community to stand against prejudice. The morning after the first reported vandalism occurred, Universal Athletics replaced the ads on their Twenty-fourth Street–facing sign with the words "Not in our town." That would become the rallying cry for several gatherings of people from all denominations to demonstrate solidarity with the Jewish community. The city's response drew national attention and recognition, was written up in several publications, and was the basis for a children's book, *The Christmas Menorah*. The following year, photographer Frederic Brenner came to Billings and photographed 240 city residents holding menorahs as a permanent record of how this city took a stand.

As the year drew to a close, Pat Bellinghausen of the *Gazette* gave her readers a glimpse into The HUB, a program of the local Mental Health Center to provide "a social center" for the mentally

The Alberta Bair Theater is home to the Billings Symphony Orchestra and a venue for traveling dramatic productions, musical events, and literary readings. KEVIN KOOISTRA-MANNING

ill in the community. Clients who frequent the HUB often come from the Montana Rescue Mission, or their own Billings homes, although some are "street people," according to Bellinghausen's article. What they find there is "recreation and therapy."[25]

A different form of recreation made news in January of 1994. The Hilands Golf Club, located in northwest Billings, was found by the state's Human Rights Commission to have violated the rights of women members by not allowing them equal access to club activities. The club agreed to redress the problems.

And again on the national scene, Billings received recognition as the third most popular destination of people who rented Ryder trucks when moving.

Some programs on the Eastern Montana College campus were moving out of Billings at the same time, however. Due to budget cuts in the Department of Defense, both the Army ROTC program and the Military Science program were dropped. (These programs were reinstated at the beginning of the 2009 academic year.)

June saw two significant cultural events. The remains of Chief Pretty Eagle and several of his fellow Crow were returned to the tribe by the American Museum of Natural History in New York. Members of the tribe gathered at Logan Field to welcome the remains with an Honor Song. The city's first Festival of Cultures was also held that month on the Rocky Mountain College campus to celebrate "cultural and ethnic diversity." This festival has become an annual event.

Eastern Montana College became Montana State University Billings in June 1994, and the following year, Dr. Ronald Sexton, a Billings native and graduate of EMC, would be named chancellor of the university, succeeding President Bruce Carpenter.

A new "unit" of state government moved to Billings this year, when the former Rivendale treatment facility became the Montana Women's Prison. Martha "Jo" Acton, a graduate of Eastern, would be named the first female warden in the state the following October.

Nineteen ninety-five saw concern over the rate of sulfur-dioxide pollution in the air over Billings, and city officials set about correcting the situation. It was, however, a busy year on the cultural front, with the Alberta Bair Theater raising $100,000 at their annual benefit, which featured Bernadette Peters, and construction starting on the expansion project at the Yellowstone Art Center.

In March, the Parmly Billings Library hosted the "Anne Frank in the World 1929–1945" exhibit for a month. There was a steady stream of visitors, including several school groups who were bused in from outlying areas.

Dorothy McLaughlin founded the Museum of Women's History in 1995 in a small room in the basement of McMullen Hall on the MSUB campus. It has since expanded and moved into quarters in downtown Billings.

In June, President Bill Clinton visited Billings. He spoke to a packed and enthusiastic crowd in the MSUB gym, went horseback riding, and dropped by the Kit Kat café in the Heights for coffee and conversation with the regulars.

Oscar Cooke, the founder and proprietor of Oscar's Dreamland, died in August—on the same day he was to be the first inductee into the National Gas and Steam Engine Hall of Fame.

Billings, along with the rest of the state, was affected by the action of the Montana legislature in December of 1995 when they dropped the posted speed limit in the state in favor of allowing drivers to proceed "in a careful and prudent manner." Unfortunately, too many people believed that they could be "careful and prudent" at 100-plus mph, and the state went back to 65 or 75 mph speed limits on highways and interstates the following year—but not before fifteen Mercedes-Benz test drivers were ticketed in July of 1996 for tearing down the interstate at 100 mph.

About the only thing moving faster than some vehicles in Montana in 1995 and '96 was methamphetamine use. Billings had a serious meth problem, and special units of both the police and sheriff's departments were formed to combat it. (Ten years later, the Montana Meth Project produced a series of hard-hitting anti-meth commercials, and meth use has dropped significantly but still remains a problem.)

June 1996 saw ZooGrass draw a crowd of more than six thousand for a performance by Martina McBride and Billings' own Wally Kurth, who is a musician as well as a well-known actor. At the same time, the movie-bug bit again, and hundreds of Billingsites stood in long lines at Metra to audition as extras in *The Horse Whisperer*, a Robert Redford film.

On a more somber note, in July the Vietnam Moving Wall replica was displayed in Pioneer Park, and hundreds of people came to pay their respects. The following month, conservators and specialists visited the Pictograph Caves south of Billings—known for years to residents as the Indian Caves—to study ways to protect the stories told there by ancient artists. Both "walls" were important reminders that the past must be honored and learned from.

Wildfires were a problem in the area throughout the summer months, and in August, homes in the Emerald Hills area of Lockwood were threatened.

Former Congressman and U.S. District Judge James Battin died in September. Battin was a graduate of Eastern Montana College. The federal building in Billings was named in his honor.

In January of 1997, a chinook—a "snow-eater" warm wind—melted the ice buildup on the Yellowstone River and caused flooding in the lowland areas of Billings. Then on the twelfth of the month, the temperature dropped precipitously to 29 below zero—a record for that date. But by February, more flooding was a problem.

February also saw the first Governor's Inaugural Ball held in Billings. (Usually such events take place in Helena, the capital city.) The reason for the break with tradition was that the new governor, Judy Martz, was a Billings native. Four thousand people attended the event.

March and April provided ample viewing opportunities as the Hale-Bopp comet streaked across the evening skies. Hale-Bopp, one of the brightest comets in modern times, delighted the people of Billings, many of whom hosted comet-watching parties, some of which were dampened a bit in early April when yet another snowstorm hit the city. (That winter set a record for snowfall—98.7 inches.)

The Billings Bulls won their second consecutive American Frontier Hockey League title in 1997, perhaps cheered on by crowds that were looking for indoor events during such a snowy season.

The weather records kept on coming, though. In June, areas near the river, including Oscar's Dreamland, were flooded when the Yellowstone rose to fifteen feet, two feet above flood stage, at Billings. On June 10, a record runoff was recorded—more than seventy cubic feet of water per second. On July 20, just to remind Billings that Mother Nature was still in charge, a storm dropped 1.6 inches of rain driven by 80 mph winds. A tornado touched down briefly near Laurel, to the west of Billings.

September saw some major changes on both Poly Drive campuses. The Bair Family Student Center was dedicated at Rocky Mountain College, and the MSU Billings College of Business moved across Poly Drive to the south into the former Professional Building. That building would later be named the Sam & Judy McDonald Family Building, honoring the McDonald family for their generous contributions to the COB.

Billings lost an important community leader in October when the Reverend Robert Freeman, eighty-one, died. He was the pastor of the Wayman Chapel. In 1993, during the stand against prejudice in Billings, Reverend Freeman voiced the thoughts of many when he said, "What hurts one of us, hurts us all."

When popular MSU Billings English professor, actor, singer, and poet Bruce Meyers died in 1992, his widow created the Poet's Garden as a permanent memorial on the campus. ROB MASSEE

Traffic on Main Street in the "Billings Heights" section suggests that Mayor Willard Fraser's idea of a tunnel through the Rims was not a bad one. ROB MASSEE

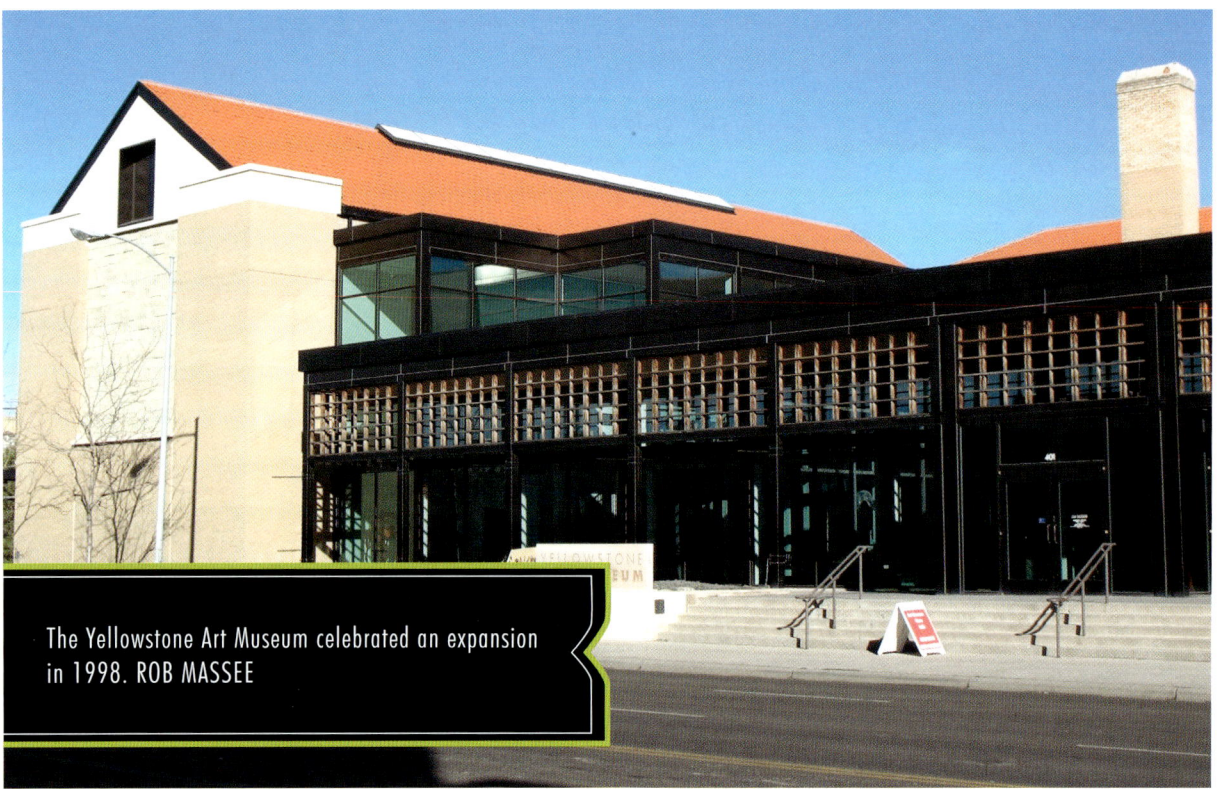

The Yellowstone Art Museum celebrated an expansion in 1998. ROB MASSEE

The Yellowstone County Veterans' Memorial on the courthouse lawn was dedicated in November, and the city had a chance to cheer when Billings West High School won its first Class AA state football championship by the slimmest of margins—34–33—over the Bozeman Hawks.

The next month, Dan Mortensen, who grew up in Billings, was named all-around champion and took his fourth World Saddle Bronc title at the National Finals Rodeo in Las Vegas.

Those winning ways continued into 1998, with Billings West repeating as state Class AA football champs, Billings Senior bringing home the boys Class AA golf title, Rocky winning the Frontier Conference Basketball crown, and Skyview taking the Class AA wrestling title.

In February of 1998, the newly named Yellowstone Art Museum opened. Director Donna Forbes, who had guided the former Art Center through the $6.2 million remodeling and addition to the original building, retired.

The following month, ground was broken for a Mormon temple in the far northwest area of the city. As what would become a new landmark in the community was beginning, an old favorite was undergoing a big change. Taxes on the Dreamland property made it necessary for Oscar Cooke's heirs to auction off most of the vehicles, tractors, antiques, etc., that had been on display there for years. Building was also in progress at the women's prison, with an industries building underway and a chapel to follow.

In July, Garth Brooks returned to Billings over the Fourth and sold out all four of his scheduled shows at Metra. Many of those who attended the western singer's shows joined the long lines of people waiting to walk through the Smithsonian's Artrain's exhibit of modern art later that month.

CHAPTER SIX BILLINGS IN THE 1980s AND '90s

St. Vincent Hospital celebrated its one-hundredth anniversary of providing medical care in Billings in August of 1998. And at the end of the year, Dan Mortensen was celebrating his fifth World Saddle Bronc title in six years.

That winning tradition in sports carried over into 1999, when Rocky Mountain College claimed its second straight Frontier Conference title in football, and the Billings Bulls won the American West Hockey League crown for the fourth year running. Billings Senior boys took home the honors in Class AA swimming, the Billings Bulls rugby team won their second straight title, and Central High swept the field in Class A boys' track. Billings Senior turned in a perfect season (14–0) on its way to claim its first state soccer championship.

Sports mania seemed to be taking over the city, with playing fields, such as the well-used Urbaska baseball park, little league teams across the city, rugby, basketball, football, swimming, and, of course, soccer. In April of 1999, Amend Park in West Billings, was putting in eight new soccer fields to join the two already established there.

In July, the school board decided to close the Garfield School and move the students enrolled there to Orchard Elementary. This was just one of what became controversial closings of other neighborhood schools due to budgetary concerns. (Record high temperatures—105 degrees on July 24—may have contributed to the heated debates.)

In the fall, the newly finished Mormon temple was opened for tours before its dedication in November. Thousands took advantage of the opportunity and enjoyed the hospitality of the Billings Mormon community during the event.

November also saw the curtain at the Alberta Bair Theater rising for the inaugural performance by the Rimrock Opera Company—a superb staging of *The Barber of Seville*.

In addition to the usual hustle and bustle of the holiday season, people in Billings—and all over the country, if not the world—were busy either stocking up on bottled water and other supplies in advance of Y2K or scoffing at those who did. Regardless of what view one took of the universal chaos that might have occurred, but didn't, with the entrance into the twenty-first century, it was a relief to wake up on January 1, 2000, to the same world it had been the day before.

Chapter SEVEN
BILLINGS IN THE TWENTY-FIRST CENTURY

DESTINATION: BILLINGS, MONTANA

The new century opened on an optimistic note after the worries about what might occur when the calendar year turned to 2000. Jim Kraft, Billings' Director of Emergency and General Services, spent all night on December 31 manning the Emergency Operations office—just in case. By January 1, however, a number of Billings' residents were ready to celebrate, which they did at the First Day Carnival at MetraPark.

The Parmly Billings Memorial Library, as a clever (and very talented) gingerbread house maker created it for the 2007 Festival of Trees, sponsored by The Family Tree, the Billings Council to Prevent Child Abuse. ROB MASSEE

The first year of the twenty-first century saw its share of problems, though. It was a dry year, prompting the Yellowstone County Commissioners to declare a "drought disaster" for agriculture in June. By July, that resolution was upgraded to a "fire emergency," with smoke reaching the city from fires near Red Lodge, on the Crow Reservation, in the Bull Mountains, and between Ashland and Broadus. By the end of the year, 2000 went on record as the worst fire season in fifty years.

The fall and winter brought problems of their own with natural gas users seeing their heating costs more than double. In December, Lockwood was designated a "Superfund" site because the groundwater was polluted with chlorinated solvents.

The Billings Symphony Orchestra celebrated its fiftieth anniversary with a special program featuring flutist James Galway. Symphony director Uri Barnea composed a commemorative piece for the occasion. And stalwarts on the cultural scene such as The Writer's Voice, Billings Studio Theater, Venture Theater, and downtown ArtWalks provided entertainment and enlightenment.

The Billings Scarlets won the state AA American Legion title, two Billings Little League teams won state titles, and the Lady Yellowjackets of MSUB made it to the NCAA Division II tournament for the fifth consecutive year.

The Heights area continued to grow, adding such new businesses as Target, Office Depot, and Wal-Mart. Downtown was doing well, also, especially in the Montana Avenue area where the former Yellowstone Garage was remodeled into a number of shops known as the "Rue des Artistes."

At the end of the year, *Gazette* business writer Jan Falstad reported on the continuing urban sprawl to the west of the city, saying that between 1990 and 1999, "24,000 acres of agricultural land had been developed around Billings."[1]

On January 17, 2001, President Bill Clinton designated Pompeys Pillar as a National Monument, getting the year off to a good start in the Billings area. Several factors were to change the mood of Billings—and the country—in the succeeding months, however.

CHAPTER SEVEN BILLINGS IN THE TWENTY-FIRST CENTURY

The Parmly Billings Library building is now home to the Western Heritage Center, an American Association of Museums accredited history museum. ROB MASSEE

Sports were a big part of the early Billings community. Max Worthington, a player for a Billings team, shows off his uniform—and his form—on a dirt playing field, 1925. WESTERN HERITAGE CENTER

Despite an earlier prohibition, casinos have sprung up all over town. Bright lights, which the City Council has been asked to curtail, flash promises of big money to passing motorists on Grand Avenue, a main east/west street. ROB MASSEE

Drought conditions continued to plague the area, and after a decade of growth, the economy began to slow down, prompting talk of recession. Three Billings elementary schools were slated for closure to enable the School Board to balance the district's budget.

None of those concerns seemed very large, however, after September 11. Sutton Sportswear printed and sold forty thousand "United We Stand" tee shirts to raise $232,000 for the Red Cross Disaster Relief Fund. A number of retired and active members of the Billings medical community volunteered their services to New York City immediately after the collapse of the towers.

There were some bright spots in 2001, of course, including the Western Heritage Center's affiliation with the Smithsonian Institution and the celebration of MetraPark's twenty-fifth year as the place where so many major community events were held. The Big Sky Fest in mid-summer brought dozens of hot air balloonists to town, as did the American Kiteflyers Association Convention in October that prompted a "Sky, Wind and World" kite exhibit at the airport. Local artist and kite builder John Pollock was instrumental in bringing the convention to Billings.

Montana's Mike Mansfield, Senate Majority Leader from 1961 to 1976 and American Ambassador to Japan for eleven years, died in October at age ninety-eight. When St. Vincent Hospital (now St. Vincent Healthcare) expanded, a new wing was named the Mansfield Center; pictures and memorabilia of Mansfield's time in Washington and Japan are displayed there.

CHAPTER SEVEN BILLINGS IN THE TWENTY-FIRST CENTURY

On November 11, the Montana Purple Heart Memorial was dedicated at the Yellowstone Courthouse, and the following month, Rocky Mountain College hosted one of three major sanctioned events in the country commemorating the sixtieth anniversary of Pearl Harbor.

Two thousand two was the fourth year of drought, and with a sluggish economy, it was a hard year for many individuals and organizations in Billings. There were some hopeful signs, however, such as a new Country Inn & Suites going up in the Heights—which, unfortunately, burned just as construction was nearing completion. Still, they were able to recover, rebuild, and open in December.

By February, the Expo Center at MetraPark had been transformed into a forty-eight-lane bowling alley, allowing Billings to host the ninety-ninth American Bowling Congress Championship Tournament, which brought $40 million worth of business into town.

Several new businesses were planning to open shop in Billings the following year—all located in the West End—including a Borders bookstore, Famous Dave's, and Montana's first Krispy Kreme (which has since closed).

The city was expanding, too, with the annexation of the Briarwood area south of town and the Cedar Park subdivision in February, the Yellowstone Country Club area in May, and the Yellowstone Country Club Estates in October. Also in October, Don and Betsey Forbes donated thirty-eight acres south of the Yellowstone Country Club to be developed as a park.

For those who enjoyed dancing, there were several opportunities, including Rocky Mountain College's annual "Black Tie & Blue Jeans" fundraiser, the Yellowstone Art Museum's first Beaux Arts Ball, and Montana State University Billings' "Dancing Through the Decades," part of the school's seventy-fifth anniversary celebration.

Sports have remained an important part of the Billings experience. American Legion teams, the Royals and the Scarlets, the MSU Billings Yellowjackets, and the Billings Mustangs, a farm league team of the Cincinnati Reds, have replaced early town baseball teams. WESTERN HERITAGE CENTER

At 272 feet, the First Interstate Bank building, built in the 1980s, is the tallest building in the state of Montana. KEVIN KOOISTRA-MANNING

On September 11, the community gathered in Pioneer Park to recognize the first anniversary of the attack on the World Trade Center and the Pentagon, and the loss of United Flight 93 near Shanksville, Pennsylvania.

In November, Billings teachers went on strike for three weeks over salaries and insurance benefits, and they weren't the only people having a hard time: Montanans' wages ranked near the lowest in the nation in 2002; stockholders of the former Montana Power Company, which had been converted to Touch America, found their once robust holdings sitting at $1 a share, and the state was struggling with a deficit of approximately $200 million.

On a cheerier note, Cleona Green and Jean Walter started Montana's first chapter of the Red Hat Society, and "The Horse of Course" fundraiser for the restoration of the Billings Depot brought in more than $450,000 through the auction of thirty-five fiberglass horses that had been decorated by local artists. Jane Waggoner Deschner was the volunteer coordinator for the project, which brightened street corners and other locations. Those painted horses can be seen on streets and in buildings all over town today.

As the year drew to a close, Billings Deaconess released its 2003 "Unsung Heroes" calendar featuring firefighters, Red Cross workers, and the like, and CTA Architects bought the Grinnell Building in downtown, which dated back to the 1920s. It had served as a hardware store from 1923 to 1954, as a plumbing outlet from 1955 to 1985, and as a grocery distribution warehouse from 1989 to 2002.

Sadly, Billings lost one of its hometown heroes in December when Dave McNally died at age sixty after battling cancer for five years.

Rocky Mountain College celebrated its 125th anniversary in 2003 with a number of commemorative events, and two Cher concerts livened up the community in the spring and summer. Venture

CHAPTER SEVEN BILLINGS IN THE TWENTY-FIRST CENTURY

The South Park natatorium provided the citizens of Billings with a first-class swimming pool when it opened in 1915. ARTHUR F. SALSBURY PHOTOGRAPH, BOB FEARS COLLECTION, WESTERN HERITAGE CENTER

The Terry Park community skating rink in the 1930s. ARTHUR F. SALSBURY PHOTOGRAPH, BOB FEARS COLLECTION, WESTERN HERITAGE CENTER

A contemporary Southside neighborhood at South Thirty-second Street. KEVIN KOOISTRA-MANNING

123

SoPo interior loft, downtown Billings, 2007. SHELLY SAUNDERS

Theater moved into larger quarters on Montana Avenue, and with several classrooms and two theaters, the program's founders, Mace Archer and Lysa Fox, were able to offer classes in dance, voice, and acting, as well as a full slate of performances. Work was also proceeding on a downtown Skatepark, scheduled to open in 2004.

The economy might have been improving on some levels, but the city was getting mixed signals. The Smith's Food store at West Park Plaza closed, leaving that shopping center with only one "anchor" store: Sears. The West End continued to expand its offerings, and downtown was picking up as well.

The weather continued to be a problem, with July 2003 the driest ever, August the second driest, and September the fourth driest since records had been kept. Between June 25 and September 30, the city recorded only .18 inches of moisture. No wonder, then, that a September fire close to town charred six hundred acres.

Intercity rivalries drew eight thousand to watch an exciting Class AA championship football game between Billings Skyview and Billings Senior in November. Skyview won the match by a score of 35 to 28 to claim the state title.

The Billings School Board decided in January of 2004 to cancel spring break in order to prepare students for the mandated No Child Left Behind tests. This was not a universally popular decision.

High school sports continued to make headlines, however. In February, Beau Malia and Joe Lauer of Skyview became the first wrestling teammates in the history of the sport in Montana to each win four consecutive state titles. Billing West's girls brought home their first Class AA swimming championship trophy, and Billings Central's boys captured the Class A swimming crown.

An exhibit of Andy Warhol's work drew record crowds to the Yellowstone Art Museum beginning in April, and in May a "farewell" concert by the Eagles sold out Metra.

The popular Athletic Park swimming pool was closed in mid-summer, leaving only three area wading pools as options for cooling off. And if the summer heat wasn't enough, more than three hundred Teamsters employed by the city struck for eleven days.

Ruth Towe, longtime director of the Moss Mansion House Museum, retired and was replaced by Joyce Mayer in September, and another historic building, the log cabin studio of famed Western artist J. Kenneth Ralston, was moved from the Rocky Mountain College campus to the grounds of the Western Heritage Center.

CHAPTER SEVEN BILLINGS IN THE TWENTY-FIRST CENTURY

The Transtech Center on Gabel Road. ROB MASSEE

The face of the city was changing in many ways, with several remodeling and/or building projects either underway or completed in 2004. Developer Steve Corning told the *Billings Gazette*'s Jan Falstad that prices of building materials had risen "significantly" over the year, but despite those increases and the rising price of land in the West End, work was continuing there as well as in downtown Billings.[2]

Billings Clinic, formerly Deaconess Hospital. ROB MASSEE

Marcia and Bill Honaker turned the site of the Sports Bar in the Securities Building into a popular restaurant, Walker's Grill, and remodeled the top floors of the building as loft apartments. Montana State University Billings, already using the former Hart Albin Building as a downtown campus, renovated and moved into the main floor of the Masonic Temple as well. And the Stapleton Building, which had once housed small shops and the popular Level Three Tea Room operated by Marie Halone, had a facelift, and now is home to condominiums and offices. By June of 2004, CTA Architects were able to move their 130 employees into the Grinnell Building, which they had purchased the year before. The old Maverick Fire Station on South Thirtieth Street was remodeled, and Smith's Funeral Home was busy redoing the former Bungalow Restaurant on South Twenty-seventh Street in order to relocate their business. In December, ground was broken for the new Temple Beth Aaron on Broadwater Avenue.

The turn-of-the-century town of Billings sprawls from east to west below Mrs. Baumgartner, who appears to be overdressed for rock climbing. WESTERN HERITAGE CENTER

From the same vantage point over one hundred years later, Tabatha Elsberry views a much larger Billings. ROB MASSEE

CHAPTER SEVEN BILLINGS IN THE TWENTY-FIRST CENTURY

The West End continued to grow, with Krispy Kreme opening as promised in July and the Transtech Center expanding. On the north side of town, the Granary Restaurant was remodeled and sold to Jon Scott and Aaron Sparboe.

In 2005, the Yegen family asked that Peter Yegen Junior's name be removed from the Peter Yegen Jr. Yellowstone County Museum. They felt that the "double name" was confusing for people. The county commissioners acceded to their request, albeit reluctantly, and most old-timers in the city still refer to the museum as "Peter Yegen's."

Michael Mace, who had been serving as interim president of Rocky Mountain College, was named president at the end of the year, and Mayor Chuck Tooley, the longest serving mayor in the history of Billings, left office after ten years of service. Tom Howard recognized Tooley's accomplishments in a front-page article in the Billings Gazette, citing his "involvement with the revitalization of the downtown area" and his "efforts to build community." Looking back on the stand the city had taken against prejudice in 1993, Tooley commented, "That showed the stuff that Billings people are made of."[3]

Tooley's successor as mayor was former Billings police chief Ron Tussing.

A SAD START TO 2006

Billings residents were saddened in January 2006 when Lieutenant Governor John Bohlinger's wife, Bette, died of leukemia. Bette and John had lived in Billings and managed Aileen's, a clothing store founded by his mother, and he had represented Billings in the state legislature for several terms, so both were well known and well liked. The following month, several of Bette's friends held a blood draw to identify bone marrow donors as a memorial to Montana's "second lady."

In 2007, Billings' football fans had the Arena Football League Billings Outlaws to entertain them—indoors.
MONICA HANSON

A "MOST VALUABLE PLAYER" AWARD

Sports made news in 2006 when Chris Valaika, Billings Mustang shortstop, achieved a thirty-one-game hitting streak and was named the league's Most Valuable Player. The Billings Outlaws won the first National Indoor Football League Championship at the MetraPark arena, and the Billings Bulls dropped from Junior A to Junior B level of hockey and joined the NorPac Hockey League. They would play in the five-hundred-seat Centennial Ice Arena in the Heights. Billings Senior took the Class AA volleyball championship, and also won the girls' Class AA cross-country title, both for the second year in a row. Montana State University Billings announced the reinstatement of baseball as a campus sport; it had been dropped in 1975 as a money-saving move.

A different kind of sport was showing up in parts of the city proper—spotting, and in some instances dodging, deer and wild turkeys looking for new habitat after their old bedding grounds were sold as building sites. The city was continuing to grow, reaching the 100,000 population mark,

The Windmill, a popular southside supper club for decades, recently moved to the Transtech Center on the west end. ROB MASSEE

and more and more new businesses were opening. Jan Falstad listed some of the additions and changes in the December 31 *Gazette*: "La Quinta, Best Western Kelly Inn & Suites, the sale of the Billings Sheraton to the Hotel Group of Washington and its renovation as the Crowne Plaza." She also noted that developer Matt Brosovich and his partners were starting construction on their "Bighorn Resort at the Shiloh Interchange, which includes a Hampton Inn & Suites, a Wingate Suite Hotel with a convention center and indoor water park, a Montana Rib and Chop House, a Wendy's, and a Holiday Gas Station." The Transtech Center added the Stapleton & Company Professional Building and became the new home of the Windmill Restaurant, long a fixture on Billings' south side.[4] Falstad also acknowledged the rapid growth in the Heights and the continuing "sprucing up" of downtown.

While some areas were booming, others were experiencing setbacks. The city's two County Markets closed, and area farmers took a hit from Mother Nature when, as Jim Gransbery reported, "a record crop of sugar beets were left frozen in the ground."[5]

Two serious fires plagued areas in and around Billings in August, including the Derby Mountain-Absarokee blaze, which grew to more than 200,000 acres and destroyed a number of homes and outbuildings, as well as wildlife and domestic animals. Emerald Hills experienced a bad burn, which destroyed the home of the new director of the Yellowstone Art Museum, Robyn Peterson, and her husband. That fire consumed 3,800 acres.

CHAPTER SEVEN BILLINGS IN THE TWENTY-FIRST CENTURY

The Billings Skate Park on South Twenty-seventh Street. ROB MASSEE

The Centennial Arena provides recreational skating opportunities for Billings residents as well as a venue for the Billings Bulls. ROB MASSEE

The Billings 1898 bowling team, the first bowling team to travel out of town for tournament play. In 2000, Billings was one of the top five cities in the United States when it came to the number of bowling alleys in operation. WESTERN HERITAGE CENTER

129

The city's baseball stadium was christened Cobb Field in honor of Robert Cobb, owner of tthe Brown Derby, who was responsible for bringing professional baseball to his hometown. Demolition of the fifty-year-old ballpark began after the final game of the 2007 season. ARTHUR F. SALSBURY PHOTOGRAPH, BOB FEARS COLLECTION, WESTERN HERITAGE CENTER

Some changes in city government occurred this year, with Rich St. John named chief of police in April and Tina Volek city administrator in August. Voters also passed a levy to build a new baseball stadium on the site of the crumbling Cobb Field.

Dehler Park, shown here under construction, opened in time for the 2008 baseball season. The first game held in the new facility was an American Legion game between Billings and Bozeman on June 29. Matt Comer of the Bozeman Bucks hit the first home run out of the new ballpark. On July 1, the first professional teams to play at Dehler took to the field. The Billings Mustangs won 9–7 over the Great Falls Voyagers, helped along by the first pro-game home run, a grand slam in the fifth inning by Mustang Michael Konstanty.

Jon Dehler, a Billings businessman, bought the naming rights for the new stadium and named Dehler Park for his father, Billy Joe Dehler, a longtime baseball fan. ROB MASSEE

The main events of the summer took place in July, the two-hundredth anniversary of William Clark's scratching his name and the date July 25, 1806, on the face of Pompeys Pillar. The Yellowstone Art Museum held its annual Summerfair, and the High Plains BookFest focused attention on the literature dealing with the Lewis & Clark expedition. But the big celebration—the Lewis & Clark Signature Event—was held at the Pillar itself over four days during which some fifty-five thousand people attended programs, visited the new Interpretative Center, and soaked up the historic atmosphere as well as the sun.

2007: BILLINGS TURNS 125

A well-known Billings woman died on March 14 in Palm Beach, Florida. For more than thirty years, Mary Alice Fortin and her husband, Philip, had generously contributed to the Billings community in a number of ways. Philip Fortin died in 1982, but his widow continued their tradition of philanthropy, funding both educational and health-related endeavors in Montana and Florida. Some examples in Billings include the Mary Alice Fortin Health Conference Center at the Billings Clinic, Fortin Lobby at St. Vincent Healthcare, and the Fortin Educational Center at Rocky Mountain College.

CHAPTER SEVEN BILLINGS IN THE TWENTY-FIRST CENTURY

Downtown Billings in 2007.
KEVIN KOOISTRA-MANNING

Our Lady of Guadalupe Church, Billings southside. ROB MASSEE

The Billings airport sees arrivals and departures from early morning until late night. ROB MASSEE

On March 15, the community officially kicked off its 125th anniversary year with a breakfast in Montana State University Billings' Student Union Ballroom. The featured speaker was Dr. Carroll Van West, a professor at Middle Tennessee University, a former director of the Western Heritage Center, and author of *Capitalism on the Frontier: Billings and the Yellowstone Valley in the Nineteenth Century*. The hundreds of community leaders in attendance were inspired by his comments on our city's past and his predictions for its future, as Lorna Thackeray noted in the *Billings Gazette*: "Several hundreds heard Carroll Van West talk about the 'civil capitalism' of early Billings. Local leaders worked together and invested in the city's future. Railroads built the town, but its founders understood it could not thrive on that basis alone."

West went on to explain that community leaders "focused on irrigation. Water turned prairies green and established another economic base," he noted. In addition, "the entire community stood behind the establishment of the city's first institution of higher learning, the Polytechnic, which would become Rocky Mountain College."

West left his audience with a challenge: "Do not be afraid to dream, because they weren't."[6]

Immediately following the kick-off event, participants were invited to visit the Western Heritage Center and tour its new exhibit, "We're Making History." That popular exhibit ran from March 15, 2007, to December 31, 2008.

CHAPTER SEVEN **BILLINGS IN THE TWENTY-FIRST CENTURY**

The Community Christmas Tree is transported from its original spot to its planting at Community Park, one of the triangle parks along Division.
ARTHUR F. SALSBURY PHOTOGRAPH, BOB FEARS COLLECTION, WESTERN HERITAGE CENTER

In 2007, the tradition of lighting the Community Tree was revived. ROB MASSEE

133

The Billings Sugar Beet Factory celebrated its centennial in 2006. ROB MASSEE

The largest church in Billings, Faith Chapel in the west end, continues to expand in both congregation and facilities. ROB MASSEE

Billings continues to grow rapidly on its west end. ROB MASSEE

Not surprisingly, the Western Heritage Center took the lead on celebrating this milestone year, offering not only its exhibits but also scheduling a series of programs covering various aspects of the community and its people.

Also in March, a well-known Billings resident received a well-deserved honor. Mike Harkins, MSUB's "winningest" basketball coach and the author of several books on basketball, was inducted into the NAIA Hall of Fame.

Renovation of historic buildings continued through this year, with architect Randy Hafer, a prime mover in restoring and refurbishing buildings in the Old Town Historic District, which he calls the "original heart of downtown," turning an 1890s building into office space on the second floor and a Subway shop on the first. The L&L building had originally housed Yee and Sam Lee's Lodging and Restaurant and, later in its life, the infamous Arcade Bar. Earlier, Hafer had restored a meat warehouse to house his High Plains Architects firm. He has been an important leader in the renovation and restoration of downtown locations.

Unfortunately, not every event of 2007 was a cause for celebration. In April, the Environmental Protection Agency (EPA) discovered underground water pollution to the southwest of downtown. According to Mike Stark of the *Billings Gazette*, "the suspected sources of PCE, a chemical found in cleaning solutions, were the Central Avenue Cleaners and Big Sky Linen."[7] And in May, a one-million-dollar fire tore through the Hi Mountain Recreation business in downtown, destroying much of the merchandise on display and filling the area with smoke.

CHAPTER SEVEN BILLINGS IN THE TWENTY-FIRST CENTURY

The new west end Fire Station No. 7 was opened in January 2008.
ROB MASSEE

The MSU Billings College of Technology on Billings west end. ROB MASSEE

St. Patrick's Co-Cathedral. ROB MASSEE

135

Pioneer Park, between Grand Avenue and Parkhill Drive, is one of many city parks. ROB MASSEE

The NILE (Northern International Livestock Exposition) Rodeo is a popular annual event at MetraPark. KEVIN KOOISTRA-MANNING

The Rex is a popular downtown restaurant and gathering spot on Montana Avenue. Gene Burgad, owner of the Rex, and Mike Schaer, president and owner of Computers Unlimited, are two central figures in the revitalization of Montana Avenue. ROB MASSEE

CHAPTER SEVEN BILLINGS IN THE TWENTY-FIRST CENTURY

The Montana Purple Heart Memorial, on the Yellowstone County Courthouse lawn, honors combat wounded veterans.
KEVIN KOOISTRA-MANNING

Throughout the summer, residents gathered in downtown Billings on Thursdays for thirteen weeks beginning in June for "Alive After Five," a gathering of young and old to enjoy music, beverages, and getting together.

In June, the Yellowstone Boys and Girls Ranch west of Billings celebrated its fiftieth year of providing residential treatment and educational opportunities to troubled youth. That same month, the Northwest Chapter of the Survivors of Bataan and Corregidor and the Third and Fourth Defense Battalion Marines gathered in Billings at the Holiday Inn for their annual reunions. A highlight of the event was the exhibit of Billings artist Ben Steele's drawing and paintings of the Bataan Death March and the POW camps he was held in for the duration of the war. The public was invited to see the exhibit, and a large number took advantage of that opportunity.

In July, the Gold Wing Road Riders Association arrived in Billings for their annual Wing Ding ("convention" to more conservative types). Approximately fourteen thousand members of the group visited Billings for the third time in the last ten years.

Conoco Phillips, one of three major oil refineries in the Billings area, is a major employer in the region. ROB MASSEE

Granite Tower is considered the technology center in downtown Billings. ROB MASSEE

CHAPTER SEVEN BILLINGS IN THE TWENTY-FIRST CENTURY

Leni Holliman was a popular broadcaster on KEMC, Billings' National Public Radio Station. KEVIN KOOISTRA-MANNING

James Kenneth, or JK, Ralston cabin, which served as both family home and studio for the well-known Western artist, was moved to the grounds of the Western Heritage Center in 2005. It now serves as a display area for his art and as a visitor center. ROB MASSEE

June, July, and August were busy months in Billings, with the Montana PRIDE parade on June 16, Summerfair in North Park, Montana Avenue Live on July 13 at the McCormick Café, the Big Sky State games in July, and both Montana Fair and the Crow Fair in August. A number of concerts were held under the SkyPoint in downtown Billings and at other venues, such as the Rex, Walker's Grill, Pug Mahon's, and the Montana Brewing Company.

Billings West High School celebrated the community's 125th year by winning the State AA basketball championship under the leadership of Coach Doug Robison, whose son Shane was one of the team's stars. The Robison family had reason to celebrate again in May when Shane was named the Midland Roundtable's male Athlete of the Year.

In October, the Parmly Billings Library Foundation celebrated Billings' 125 years by inaugurating the High Plains Book Awards, given in conjunction with the High Plains BookFest. Awards were given at a banquet on the MSUB campus, with the Emeritus Award, given for a body of work, going to Larry Watson, author of *Montana 1948* and *White Crosses*.

All through the year, of course, the Billings community had been celebrating in ways large and small the pleasure of living in this big—for Montana—city at the base of the Rimrocks, which still honors its founders and strives to improve on the foundation they provided us.

notes

CHAPTER ONE BILLINGS IN THE NINETEENTH CENTURY

1. C. Adrian Heidenreich, Ph.D. "History of Indian Religion in Montana." *Religion in Montana*, ed. Lawrence F. Small, 1–45. (Billings, MT: Rocky Mountain College, 1992).
2. Joyce M. Jensen. *Pieces & Places of Billings History* (Billings: Western Heritage Press, 1994), 19.
3. Western Heritage Center storyboard.
4. Sue Hart. *The Call to Care* (Billings: St. Vincent Hospital, 1998), 18.
5. *Billings Herald*, October 8, 1882.
6. Ibid.
7. Ibid.
8. Ibid.
9. *Billings Herald*, October 12, 1882.
10. *Billings Gazette*, October 5, 1892.
11. Hart, *The Call to Care*, 42.
12. Western Heritage Center storyboard.
13. Karen D. Stevens and Dee Ann Redman. *Billings A to Z* (Billings: Friends of the Library, 1995), 35.
14. Rick Underwood, *Billings Gazette*, Centennial Edition, 1989.
15. Ben Steele, Sr., as told to Shirley Steele, 1971.

CHAPTER TWO BILLINGS IN THE EARLY TWENTIETH CENTURY

1. Hart, *The Call to Care*, 19.
2. *Billings Daily Journal*, March 25, 1908.
3. *Billings Daily Journal*, evening edition, March 27, 1908.
4. Dale Eunson, *Up on the Rim* (Helena: Riverbend Publishing, 2002), 162.
5. Louis Lundborg, *Up to Now* (New York: Norton, 1978), 77.
6. Ibid., 90.
7. *Weekly Bulletin*, December 27, 1911.
8. Ibid.
9. Ibid.
10. Ibid.
11. Ibid.
12. Ibid.
13. Ibid.
14. Gwendolen Haste. "Pattern of Time," unpublished manuscript.
15. Ibid.
16. Ibid.
17. Ibid.

CHAPTER THREE BILLINGS IN THE 1920S AND '30S

1. Western Heritage Center clipping file.
2. *Billings Gazette*, July 4, 1927.
3. Ibid.
4. Ibid.
5. Ibid.
6. *Billings Gazette*, November 28, 1928.
7. Ibid.
8. *Yellowstone*. Western Heritage clipping file.
9. Courtesy of Lee Ann MacDonald Bourcier.
10. Ibid.
11. *Stanolind Record*, January 1931, 14.
12. Christene C. Meyers. *Billings Gazette*, Centennial Edition.
13. *Billings Gazette*, September 17, 1960.
14. *Billings Gazette*, July 27, 1936.
15. Julie Coleman. *Golden Opportunities: A Biographical History of Montana's Jewish Communities*. (Helena, MT: Distributed by Falcon Press, c1994).
16. Hart, *The Call to Care*, 57.
17. Stevens and Redman, *Billings A to Z*, 10.
18. Christene C. Meyers, *Billings Gazette*, Centennial Edition, 16.

CHAPTER FOUR BILLINGS IN THE 1940S AND '50S

1. *Billings Gazette*, September 13, 1940.
2. Ibid.
3. *Billings Gazette*, May 13, 1943.
4. Ibid.

5. *Billings Gazette*. April 18, 1941.
6. *Billings Gazette*, April 19, 1941.
7. Gary Glynn. *Montana's Home Front During World War II* (Missoula, MT: Pictorial Histories Publishing Company, Inc., 1992), 53.
8. Ibid., 75.
9. Addison Bragg. *Writers Under the Rims: a Yellowstone County Anthology*, ed. Sue Hart et al. (Billings: Parmly Billings Library Foundation, 2001), 82.
10. Glynn, 76.
11. Ibid., 162.
12. Ibid., 182.
13. Ibid.
14. Ibid., 13.
15. Ibid., 116.
16. *Billings Gazette*, July 4, 1943.
17. Glynn, 140.
18. Ibid., 202.
19. Stevens and Redman, *Billings A to Z*, 38.
20. Ibid., 92.
21. *Billings Gazette*, October 5, 1955.
22. Kim Larsen, *Billings Gazette*, July 23, 1989.
23. *Billings Gazette*, December 29, 1957.
24. Ibid.
25. Ibid.
26. Ibid.
27. Western Heritage Center storyboard.
28. *Billings Gazette*, July 4, 1958.
29. Western Heritage Center storyboard.
30. *Billings Gazette*, August 18, 1959.

CHAPTER FIVE BILLINGS IN THE 1960S AND '70S

1. Sam Blythe. *Billings Gazette*, January 1, 1961.
2. *Billings Gazette*, January 1, 1961.
3. Ibid.
4. *Billings Gazette*, October 9, 1960.
5. *Billings Gazette*, January 1, 1963.
6. *Billings Gazette*, January 1, 1965.
7. *Billings Gazette*, December 29, 1967.
8. Christene C. Meyers, *Billings Gazette*, April 12, 1970.
9. Kathryn Wright, *Billings Gazette*, August 13, 1969.
10. Stevens and Redman, *Billings A to Z*, 18.
11. Roger Clawson, *Billings Gazette*, September 20, 1972.
12. Kerry Pechter, *Billings Gazette*, December 24, 1976.
13. Stevens and Redman, *Billings A to Z*, 39.
14. Ibid., 26.

CHAPTER SIX BILLINGS IN THE 1980S AND '90S

1. *Billings Gazette*, July 14, 1981.
2. *Billings Gazette*, June 18, 1982.
3. *Billings Gazette*, September 18, 1982.
4. *Billings Gazette*, August 13, 1982.
5. Mark Ragan, *Billings Gazette*, December 15, 1982.
6. Mark Ragan, *Billings Gazette*, January 4, 1983.
7. Christene C. Meyers, *Billings Gazette*, March 14, 1983.
8. *Billings Gazette*, April 12, 1983.
9. Mark Ragan, *Billings Gazette*, April 12, 1983.
10. *Billings Gazette*, December 23, 1984.
11. Stevens and Redman, *Billings A to Z*, 70.
12. *Billings Gazette*, December 28, 1984.
13. Kim Larsen, *Billings Gazette*, December 8, 1985.
14. *Billings Gazette*, December 30, 1985.
15. *Billings Gazette*, December 18, 1986.
16. *Billings Gazette*, December 26, 1986.
17. Paul Holley, *Billings Gazette*, December 25, 1986.
18. *Billings Gazette*, December 19, 1987.
19. *Billings Gazette*, December 22, 1987.
20. *Billings Gazette*, December 22, 1988.
21. *Billings Gazette*, August 31, 1989.
22. Kim Larsen, *Billings Gazette*, September 4, 1989.
23. Vickie McLaughlin, *Billings Gazette*, September 6, 1989.
24. *Billings Gazette*, December 28, 1993.
25. Pat Bellinghausen, *Billings Gazette*, December 26, 1993.

CHAPTER SEVEN BILLINGS IN THE TWENTY-FIRST CENTURY

1. Jan Falstad, *Billings Gazette*, December 31, 2000.
2. Jan Falstad, *Billings Gazette*, December 26, 2004.
3. Tom Howard, *Billings Gazette*, December 30, 2005.
4. Jan Falstad, *Billings Gazette*, December 31, 2006.
5. Jim Gransbery, *Billings Gazette*, December 31, 2006.
6. Lorna Thackeray, *Billings Gazette*, March 16, 2007.
7. Mike Stark, *Billings Gazette*, April 3, 2007.

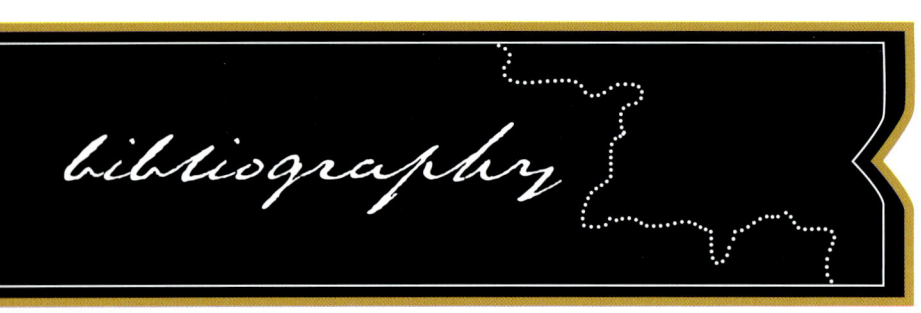

bibliography

Billings Gazette. Issues from 1885 to present.

Billings Herald, 1882.

Billings Journal, 1908.

Coleman, Julie L. *Golden Opportunities*. Helena, Mont.: Falcon Press, 1994.

DeCosse, Mildred Dover. *The Man of Dover's Island*. New York: Carlton Press, 1973.

Eunson, Dale. *Up on the Rim*. New York: Farrar, Straus & Giroux, 1970.

Glynn, Gary. *Montana's Home Front During World War II*. Missoula, Mont.: Pictorial Histories Publishing Company, Inc.,1992.

Hart, Sue. *The Call to Care*. Billings, Mont.: St. Vincent Healthcare, 1998.

———. *Yellow-stone & Blue*. Billings: Montana State University–Billings, 2002.

Hart, Sue, Donna Davis, Ken Egan Jr., and Joyce Jensen, eds. *Writers Under the Rims*. Billings, Mont.: Parmly Billings Library Foundation, 2001.

Haste, Gwendolen. "Pattern of Time." Unpublished manuscript, n.d. Copy in collection of the author.

Jensen, Joyce M. *Pieces & Places of Billings History*. Billings, Mont.: Western Heritage Press, 1994.

Lundborg, Louis. *Up to Now*. New York: Norton, 1978.

Small, Lawrence F., ed. *Religion in Montana*. Billings, Mont.: Rocky Mountain College, 1992.

Stanoline Record, January 1931.

Steele, Ben, Sr. "Billings in the 1890s." Unpublished manuscript as told to Shirley Steele. Copy in collection of the author.

Stevens, Karen D., and Dee Ann Redman. *Billings A to Z*. Billings, Mont.: Friends of the Library, 1995.

Weekly Bulletin, 1911.

Western Heritage Center clippings file.

Western Heritage Center storyboards.

Yellowstone. Worden, Montana.

index

Allard, Louis, 40, 43, 60

Babcock, A. L., 14, 17

Babcock, Gov. Tim, 87, 88

Bair, Charlie, 14, 15, 51, 52

Barnea, Uri, 118

Billings, Frederick, 14, 18, 21, 100, 109

Billings, Frederick, Jr., 28

Billings, Parmly, 15, 18, 28

Billings Midland Club, 48

Camp, Mrs. Edgar B., 14

Canary, Martha Jane, 18

Chapple, Henry, 21, 22

Cobb Field, 79, 81, 91, 130

Community Christmas Tree, 133

Covert, Helen, 61

Coxey's Army, 25

Deaconess Hospital, 48, 49, 50, 82, 105, 106, 122, 125

Depression years, 54–55, 59

Earhart, Amelia, 61

Eunson, Dale, 34, 35

Foote, Stella, 77, 81, 92

Fortin, Mary Alice, 64, 130

Fortin, Phillip, 64, 130

Fraser, Willard, 91, 94, 95, 103, 113

Hafer, Randy, 21, 134

Hart, William S., 50, 51, 52

Haste, Gwendolen, 36, 42, 44, 45

Hemingway, Ernest, 60

Kennedy, John F., 88

KKK, 50

Lindbergh, Charles, 52, 54

Logan, Della Mae, 76

Logan, Dick, 54

Losekamp, John D., 17, 18, 24

Lundborg, Louis, 35, 36, 37

MacDonald, William Melville, 57, 59

Maverick Hose Company, 18

McCormick, Paul, 17, 18, 81, 100

McMullen, Dr. Lynn, 49, 75

Midland Empire Fair, 43, 55, 57

Moss, P. B., 14, 22, 29, 31, 32, 36, 70

Newman, O. N., 25

Normal School, 48, 49, 50, 62, 75

Northern Hotel, 14, 15, 32, 39, 44, 70–73, 87

O'Donnell, I. D., 14, 15, 22, 30, 31

Phillis Wheatley Club, 94

Polio epidemics, 39, 40, 48, 78

Polytechnic Institute, 18, 39, 41

Pompeys Pillar, 81, 118, 130

Rolle, Marjorie Logan, 62

Rowley, Henry, 14, 15, 22, 30, 31, 32

St. Vincent Hospital, 15, 22, 28, 29, 40, 48, 49, 50, 55, 60, 64, 70, 73, 78, 81, 82, 88, 115, 120, 130

Steele, Ben, Jr., 23, 127

Steele, Ben, Sr., 23, 25

Temple Beth Aaron, 64, 125

Tooley, Chuck, 127

Warren, Olive, 18, 19

Webb, James, 33–34

West, Dr. Carroll Van, 132

Wright, Kathryn, 76, 100

World War I, 36, 39, 48, 54, 74

World War II, 62, 75, 76, 77, 78, 80

Yale Oil, 55, 63–64, 79

Yegen, Christian, 14, 17, 22, 24, 54

Yegen, Peter, 14, 17, 22, 24, 54

Yegen, Peter, Jr., 25, 81, 127

Yellowstone Hurrah!, 101

Zimmerman, Joseph, 21, 24

Zimmerman Trail, 21, 45

ABOUT THE author

Sue Hart teaches in the English and Philosophy Department at Montana State University–Billings. She is the author of The Call to Care, the history of St. Vincent Hospital, and Yellow-Stone & Blue, a history of the first seventy-five years of Montana State University–Billings. She has written numerous articles about Montana authors and their works and other Montana subjects, and makes frequent presentations around the state on literary topics. She was the scriptwriter and a co-producer of a MontanaPBS documentary on Dorothy M. Johnson, Gravel in Her Gut & Spit in Her Eye, a finalist for the 2006 Spur Award given by Western Writers of America, and was an associate-producer of Paradise & Purgatory: Hemingway at the L–T and St. Vincent Hospital, also a MontanaPBS documentary. She is the recipient of a Governor's Award in the Humanities, a Governor's Award for AIDS Education, the Montana Historical Society's Trustees Educator's Award, a PEN Award for Syndicated Fiction, and, most recently, a WILLA Award for creative nonfiction. She raised her four children, Kathleen, Mary, Michael, and Margaret, in Billings, and is married to author Richard S. Wheeler, winner of five Spur Awards and the Owen Wister Award for outstanding contributions to the literature of the West from Western Writers of America.